Reminiscences
of the
Santiago Campaign

Also from Westphalia Press
westphaliapress.org

The Idea of the Digital University

Dialogue in the Roman-Greco World

The History of Photography

International or Local Ownership?:
Security Sector Development in
Post-Independent Kosovo

Lankes, His Woodcut Bookplates

Opportunity and Horatio Alger

The Role of Theory in Policy Analysis

The Little Confectioner

Non-Profit Organizations and Disaster

The Idea of Neoliberalism: The
Emperor Has Threadbare
Contemporary Clothes

Social Satire and the Modern Novel

Ukraine vs. Russia: Revolution,
Democracy and War: Selected Articles
and Blogs, 2010-2016

James Martineau and
Rebuilding Theology

A Strategy for Implementing the
Reconciliation Process

Issues in Maritime Cyber Security

A Different Dimension: Reflections on
the History of Transpersonal Thought

Iran: Who Is Really In Charge?

Contracting, Logistics, Reverse
Logistics: The Project, Program and
Portfolio Approach

Unworkable Conservatism: Small
Government, Freemarkets, and
Impracticality

Springfield: The Novel

Lariats and Lassos

Ongoing Issues in Georgian Policy
and Public Administration

Growing Inequality: Bridging
Complex Systems, Population Health
and Health Disparities

Designing, Adapting, Strategizing in
Online Education

Pacific Hurtgen: The American Army
in Northern Luzon, 1945

Natural Gas as an Instrument of
Russian State Power

New Frontiers in Criminology

Feeding the Global South

Beijing Express: How to Understand
New China

The Rise of the Book Plate: An
Exemplative of the Art

Reminiscences of the Santiago Campaign

The Spanish-American War of 1898

by John Bigelow, Jr.

WESTPHALIA PRESS
An Imprint of Policy Studies Organization

Westphalia Press
An imprint of Policy Studies Organization
1527 New Hampshire Ave., NW
Washington, D.C. 20036
info@ipsonet.org

ISBN-13: 978-1-63391-648-7
ISBN-10: 1-63391-648-0

Cover design by Jeffrey Barnes:
jbarnesbook.design

Daniel Gutierrez-Sandoval, Executive Director
PSO and Westphalia Press

Updated material and comments on this edition
can be found at the Westphalia Press website:
www.westphaliapress.org

Reminiscences
of the
Santiago Campaign

By

JOHN BIGELOW, Jr.

CAPTAIN 10TH U. S. CAVALRY

AUTHOR OF "THE PRINCIPLES OF STRATEGY"

WITH A MAP

NEW YORK AND LONDON
HARPER & BROTHERS PUBLISHERS
1899

CONTENTS

CHAP.   PAGE

PREFACE   V

I. JOINING THE REGIMENT   1

II. CAMP THOMAS, GEORGIA   9

III. BY RAIL TO LAKELAND, FLORIDA 27

IV. IN CAMP AT LAKELAND 36

V. TO TAMPA BAY AND EMBARKATION 44

VI. ON TRANSPORT IN TAMPA BAY 55

VII. AT SEA 70

VIII. DAIQUIRI 78

IX. LAS GUASIMAS 88

X. SEVILLA 93

XI. EL POZO 103

XII. UNDER FIRE 108

XIII. SAN JUAN 120

XIV. WOUNDED 129

XV. IN DIVISION HOSPITAL 138

XVI. IN GENERAL HOSPITAL 142

XVII. TO TAMPA BAY AND FORT MCPHERSON, GEORGIA 147

XVIII. CONVALESCENCE 156

XIX. RETURN TO DUTY 158

XX. CONCLUSION 165

PREFACE

ON my return from the Cuban campaign in July last, I found the community into which I was thrown during my convalescence intensely interested in every detail of the experience of any one who had participated in it. The space subsequently given in the public prints to the proceedings of the President's Commission for Inquiring into the Conduct of the War, has led my friends as well as some publishers to urge me to allow the general public to share such information about the campaign as my observation and experience enables me to impart. It is in deference to these considerations that these pages, revised from my correspondence with my family, are now submitted to the public. They make no pretension to be a history of the late war, nor even of the campaign of Santiago, but simply what the title implies—a narration of what an officer participating in that campaign saw, felt, and thought, with such explanations and suggestions as his observations and reflections prompted.

PREFACE

The enlisting, organizing, drilling, and equipping of an army of over two hundred and fifty thousand men, the transportation of about twenty thousand of them to a theatre of war a thousand miles or more distant, and from a temperate to a tropical climate, on less than one month's notice for preparation, involved endless confusion and an almost total disregard of the rules and precautions of scientific warfare. In this narration I have not sought to give undue prominence to, still less to disguise, any of the consequences of this want of preparation. On the contrary, if what I have to report can have any value, professionally or otherwise, and I hope it will be found to have some, it must consist mainly in the frank disclosure of everything that fell under my personal observation, the recurrence of which our Government in the future should strive to avoid.

Neither have I presumed to assess or distribute any one's share of responsibility for what was amiss. There are proper tribunals for the discharge of that delicate and ungracious duty which, without extenuating culpable abuses or wanton neglect, may be expected to make due allowance for the suddenness with which the pending war was precipitated upon the country. These abuses and neglects are liable to be obscured by the surprising results of the war, due more, perhaps, to the unsuspected weakness of

PREFACE

the enemy than to the strategic skill of our commanders.   It seems the more desirable, therefore,
that every one who took part in this war should
give the Government and the public the benefit
of his observations.   It is as wise to learn from
our friends as from our enemies.

J. B., JR.

FORT CLARK, Texas, *February* 13, 1899.

REMINISCENCES

OF THE

SANTIAGO CAMPAIGN

I

JOINING THE REGIMENT

THE gathering of the war clouds and our declaration of war found me at the Massachusetts
Institute of Technology, Boston, discharging the
duties of a "Professor of Military Science and
Tactics." Officers of the Regular Army on detached service were being ordered to rejoin their
regiments; many had applied for such orders.
For my part, I thought it improper for a regular
soldier to volunteer unless volunteers were called
for. I accordingly abstained for what seemed to
me a long time from making an application for
active service. At length I read in the papers
that transports were being assembled at Tampa,
and that the colored troops, of which my regiment

formed a part, were pretty sure to be all ordered
to Cuba with the first expedition. Still my
orders did not come. I observed that while the
other colored regiments were moved East, the
Tenth Cavalry was left in its posts in Montana.
At last I saw it reported that the Tenth Cavalry
was ordered to Chickamauga Park, and troops
were being assembled at Tampa, Florida, to be
formed into a corps of invasion. Fearing that
the Tenth Cavalry might be moved down there
and shipped to Cuba without me, I wrote to the
Adjutant-General of the army, requesting that
I be ordered to join my regiment. Next day I received the following letter:

WAR DEPARTMENT,
ADJUTANT-GENERAL'S OFFICE,
WASHINGTON, *April* 28, 1898.

Captain John Bigelow, Jr., Tenth Cavalry,
    Through the President of the Massachusetts Institute of
    Technology, Boston, Massachusetts :

    SIR,—I have the honor to inform you that orders have
been issued relieving you from your present duties at the
Massachusetts Institute of Technology. While the ex-
igencies of the times render this necessary, it is the intention of the War Department to return you to the
Institution, from which you are now withdrawn, at the
opening of the next scholastic year, if your services shall
become available for that purpose.

Very respectfully,
THEO. SCHWANN,
Assistant Adjutant-General.

JOINING THE REGIMENT

The following day I received my order:

Special Orders, HEADQUARTERS OF THE ARMY,
No. 99. ADJUTANT-GENERAL'S OFFICE,
WASHINGTON, *April* 28, 1898.

[Extract.]

* * * * * * *

23. By direction of the President, Captain John Bigelow, Jr., Tenth Cavalry, is relieved, by the Secretary of War, from duty at the Massachusetts Institute of Technology, Boston, Massachusetts, and will proceed to join his troop. The travel enjoined is necessary for the public service.

* * * * * * *

By command of MAJOR-GENERAL MILES.
H. C. CORBIN, Adjutant-General.

The order did not state where my regiment was, so I had to reflect and plan a little before proceeding to its execution. I had never received any official information of a movement of the regiment or any part of it from where I left it when I came East—Fort Custer and Fort Assinniboine, Montana—months before. I did not know whether the regiment had arrived at Chattanooga, or, having arrived there, had gone on to Tampa or elsewhere. But I was ordered from the headquarters of the army to join my troop.* As I

* A regiment of cavalry consists of twelve troops. At this time two troops (L and M) of each regiment were "skeletons"—that is, they had no enlisted men, and their officers were on detached service. Skeleton troops existed only on paper.

3

belonged to a skeleton troop, I would have been puzzled, had I stopped to think about it, as to how I was actually to connect myself with the airy nothing of which I was nominally Captain; for I did not expect to find any of the officers of my troop serving as attached to a soldierless organization. But I did not anticipate that difficulty. My thoughts were upon the larger and primary purpose of finding my regiment. I determined to go to Washington and get on its trail. Before doing so, I had to devote some time to closing up my affairs at the Institute of Technology, and to fitting myself out for field-service. My efforts in the latter direction made me realize as I had never realized before that I was a military man in an unmilitary country. A British officer, ordered to foreign parts, has only to step into, or communicate with, the officers' co-operative store in London to provide himself with a complete outfit—clothing, arms, camp-furniture, etc.—for service in any part of the world at any season of the year. There is no establishment in the United States—at least, none known to me—where an American officer can do that.

At the time of which I am writing there was no uniform known to our army that was suitable for service in the tropics. I had reason to believe that one was being devised at Washington, but I did not know when it would be prescribed and adopted. I thought it necessary, therefore,

4

to complete my cloth undress uniform by pro-
viding myself with a pair of riding-trousers, campaign hat, gauntlets, and riding-leggings. The
trousers cost me twice as much as they would
have cost at a military post, and did not fit me.
The cutter evidently went on the theory that
riding-trousers are simply walking-trousers cut
short and made to stick into a pair of boots. I
did not know where to get a regulation campaign
hat, except from the Quartermaster's Department of the United States Army. The red tape
necessary to do that from Boston staggered me.
I decided to wait until I found my regiment,
trusting that I would find somewhere in its vicinity a depot at which I could purchase not
only a campaign hat, but also a pair of gauntlets
and riding-leggings. I had no mess outfit, but
expected that I would find a mess already running in the troop to which I should be assigned,
and, if not, that I would be able to purchase one
from some other officer or from a dealer. I hoped
likewise to provide myself on the spot with a cot,
chairs, table, and other camp-furniture.

I left Boston on a night train, Sunday, the
1st of May. As I made my way next morning
through the grand building of the State, War,
and Navy Departments, to the office of the Adjutant-General, I found the halls and stairways
alive with a motley crowd. I was struck by certain male couples, the individuals of which con-

trasted strangely with each other, one being elderly and evidently experienced in the ways of the world, especially along the lines of politics; the other young and fresh, with an air of blended hope and trustfulness which bespoke a protégé being initiated into the mysteries of army promotion. On passing through the door which I thought admitted me to the presence of the Adjutant-General, I was confronted by one of his assistants who, after returning my salutation, informed me that he was very busy, asked me what he could do for me, and, on being informed, referred me to a clerk, and gave me his messenger as a guide. The clerk informed me that my regiment was at Chickamauga, but by the time I got there might be somewhere else, as troops were being moved pretty briskly, especially between Chickamauga and Tampa. He advised me to telegraph to my regimental Adjutant for instructions as to where I should go to join the regiment, and I acted on his advice.

I finally received the following answer to my telegram:

CHICKAMAUGA PARK, Georgia, *May 2,* 1898.
Captain Jno. A. Bigelow, U. S. A., Washington, D. C.:
Regimental commander directs that you join regiment at Chickamauga.
BARNUM, Adjt.

An officer travelling under orders was at that time allowed transportation in kind (fare and sleeper) and mileage at the rate of four cents a mile.* The quartermaster at Boston had given me transportation to Washington. The quartermaster at Washington gave me transportation to Lytle, Georgia, the nearest station to Chickamauga Park, where my regiment was camped. My mileage I could not collect until I had completed my journey.

Leaving Washington that evening, I reached Chattanooga the following evening. At the station I saw a tall, fine-looking cavalryman, whom I recognized as Sergeant Ray, Color-Sergeant of the Tenth Cavalry, and learned from him that there was no train to Lytle that would get me there much before midnight. Had I been young and inexperienced, I would doubtless have waited for a train and gone out to camp that night. I would have found everybody asleep, and had to wake some one up to be admitted to a tent. The next morning I would have startled the Colonel by my early appearance and been laughed at by many of my brother officers for my extraordinary zeal. Anticipating all this, I took a hack and drove to what the driver asserted was the best hotel in town. I found there a number of officers of my regiment and of other regular regiments. There were no

---

* He is now allowed mileage at the rate of seven cents a mile to cover all expenses.

volunteers at this time in the camp to which I was going.

On the morning of May 4th I took the train for Lytle. As I passed Lookout Mountain and Missionary Ridge, and recalled the feats of arms which made those heights historical, I contemplated in my mind's eye something of the same order beyond the seas.

The station of Lytle was surrounded with shops, booths, store-houses, etc., called into existence by the great camp near by. Officers and soldiers, teamsters, wagons, ambulances, and riding-horses were on every hand. If I remember rightly, I rode to the headquarters of the Tenth Cavalry by the side of the driver of an escort wagon.

II

As I had apprehended, I found that my own troop (M) had not assumed material form. The Colonel assigned me to Troop D. I had commanded this troop for a short time, years before. The term of service had been shortened since then, and there were none of the men of that day in the troop. But to my great satisfaction I found that the First Sergeant was William H. Givens, whom I remembered as a sergeant in Troop B when I joined it fresh from West Point in 1877, and as First Sergeant of Troop K while I served in that organization several years later. We had followed many a long, dry trail together in Texas and Arizona. The two lieutenants whom I found with the troop I had never met before. My First Lieutenant was soon detailed as recruiting-officer in Chattanooga, leaving me my Second Lieutenant, J. F. Kennington, a West Point graduate of 1896, who had recently, in the absence of the First Lieutenant as well as of the Captain, commanded the troop for some time. His knowledge of the men and affairs

9

of the troop made his services peculiarly valuable.

About the first thing I did on assuming command was to take an inventory of the property in the hands of the men. I made a blank form, with the roster of the troop in a column on the left-hand side, and the articles constituting the kit on a line at the top, with four columns for each article. Armed with this sheet, and accompanied by the First Sergeant, I went through each squad in succession, checking each article opposite each name as here indicated :

> S—serviceable.
> R—to be repaired in troop.
> C—to be condemned.
> M—missing.

The articles to be repaired were mostly saddlery. They were pointed out to the chiefs of squads, who were charged with seeing that the men responsible for them took them to the troop saddler and had them repaired. The articles to be condemned were placed on inventory and inspection reports. Finally, requisitions were made out for articles to replace those which were to be condemned and those which were missing. The inventory and inspection reports were acted on several weeks later in another camp. The requisitions had soon to be made over again, because, as I understood, they were lost at division headquarters. Even this second edition was practically never filled. The bulk of what it called for was received, I believe, in the detention camp at Montauk Point, after the campaign of Santiago.

Supplies kept coming to the regiment at intervals in insufficient quantity to supply the whole regiment. Whenever they came they were divided among the several troops. Each troop was continually receipting for driblets of what it needed, and was never fully supplied. If a force of from fifty to one hundred men armed and equipped for field-service were called for, it had to be made up from several troops. This, I think, might have been obviated by issuing supplies from regimental headquarters to a single troop at a time, or such number of troops as could be fully supplied.

Many of the men had no rubber overcoats or slickers (oiled canvas coats like sou'westers), there was no prospect of any being furnished by the government, and the Quartermaster's Department did not even have such an article for sale. Understanding that it was important for foreigners in the tropics to keep dry, and although I did not believe that a campaign would be started in Cuba until after the " rainy season," I took steps at once to procure slickers for the men who needed and wanted them. This I could only do by getting them to contribute three dollars of their pay per man, and arranging to buy the garments of a private firm. These arrangements, however, were very slow of consummation, and the men interested in them were destined to go to Cuba without slickers. I provided for myself by going to Chattanooga and buying a rubber overcoat.

There was no sign of a summer uniform. Men and officers were wearing the uniforms which they wore through the winter in Montana, except that they commonly left off their blouses. The blue shirt of the enlisted men looked trim and soldierly enough without suspenders, which they were generally prohibited from wearing on duty. But without suspenders they had difficulty in keeping up their trousers. The Quartermaster's Department, it seems to me, might issue suspenders of the color of the blouse, and the men be allowed to wear them on duty. I saw officers going about on duty and off duty, without blouses and without suspenders, in white shirts, blue shirts, and parti-colored shirts. Officers and non-commissioned officers, as a rule, when they left off their blouses had no insignia of rank about them except the stripes on their trousers. It was consequently hard, and often impossible, to distinguish an officer from a sergeant. I heard of one organization—I think it was the First Cavalry—in which the officers were not allowed to do duty in shirts or without

blouses on. Many of the officers provided themselves with flannel abdominal bandages to wear
in the tropics. I bought one myself, but never
wore it.

It may have been due to my long absence
from the Regular Army and my association with
militia and college soldiers, but I was strongly
impressed by the soldierly bearing of the men in
and out of ranks. The set-up and discipline of
the enlisted men seemed better than when I left
my regiment four years before. The officers of
the regiment were generally younger and more
efficient than at that time. But they impressed
me as lacking in discipline. More than once I
saw an officer "attend stables" or superintend
the grooming of the horses of a troop, sitting on
a bale of hay smoking a cigarette and reading a
newspaper.

In one squadron there was a school for non-
commissioned officers in picket and outpost duty.
But there was no instruction of that sort, theoretical or practical, for officers.

Camp George H. Thomas, as our camp was
called, was to me a great disappointment. I expected to find it a camp of instruction, in which
advance and rear guard service, the tactics of infantry, cavalry, and artillery, separately and combined, would be illustrated and taught practically
on a large scale. I expected to find the camp
covered with pickets as it would be in the pres-

ence of the enemy, and to take my regular turn at outpost duty, to practice patrolling and reconnoitring beyond the outposts, to see large bodies of troops manœuvre against each other and deploy, and go through the forms of an attack and defence. I saw nothing of the kind. Most of the drilling that I did was by company or troop. I participated in a few squadron and regimental drills, but saw nothing in the nature of a field-exercise. Towards the latter part of our stay in this camp, the troop commanders were directed to devote a portion of the drill to instruction in advance and rear guard and outpost duty. But what could one do in this way with a force little larger than a good-sized patrol or picket? I heard of there having been four and five hours of drill a day, but I never drilled more than three hours a day myself, and did all the drilling that I was required to do, and properly could do. During our last two days in camp we drilled but about an hour and a half a day.

The camp was pitched upon the old battle-field of Chickamauga, now Chickamauga Park. Chickamauga Station is about six miles from Lytle. Both Lytle and Chickamauga Station adjoin the park. Our regiment occupied part of an open space on a gently sloping hill-side. A wood of large trees limited the view at the top and bottom of the slope. From near the top the tents of our field and staff officers looked down on the line of tents of the troop officers and the lines of tents or streets of the several troops. About half a mile to our right was another regiment of cavalry, and about three-quarters of a mile to our left and front, hidden by the woods from our view, was a regiment of infantry. The details of our camp were substantially those prescribed in the drill regulations. The garbage was disposed of by throwing it into a hole about $4 \times 6 \times 6$ and covering it daily with a few inches of earth. This hole was about twenty feet from the cook fire. Portions were burned in the cook fire. The manure was carted into the woods, about two hundred yards from the picket-line, and dumped there. The drinking-water was obtained from a hydrant, and seemed to be good. Water for washing was kept in barrels in each troop. It was common, however, for men to drink it.

Back of our camp was a tower from which tourists could obtain a commanding view of the battle-field of Chickamauga, and all through the grounds were monuments, tablets, and other helps and inspirations to a study of the battle. But I had little time or energy for reading or sight-seeing. The camp was so far from any stream suitable for bathing that I had to buy tubs for my men, paying for them out of the company fund. Most of the bathing was done after dark, there being but one small tent to bathe in during the day. The dirty water was poured over the surface of the ground. Once the whole squadron was marched, mounted, to a point on a stream about six miles distant, and the men treated to a swim. No. 4 of each set of fours held the horses of Nos. 1, 2, and 3, until one of the latter had bathed and returned. The water was pretty cold, but the men enjoyed it, splashing and shouting like a lot of small boys. It was a fine opportunity to study the physique of the colored soldiers, and many were the admiring comments made by the officers, who watched them with a good deal of interest and not a little envy. The command went back to camp at a brisk trot.

Regarding the completion of my personal outfit, I found there was practically nothing to be gotten by purchase or otherwise from the government or from individual officers. My Lieutenant was messing with the officers of another troop, and had no mess outfit of his own. After some deliberation and inquiry, I sent an order to Ettenson, Woolfe & Co., of Leavenworth, Kansas, for their "bucket-mess outfit," which I received in due time, and found it to be the best thing of its kind that I have ever known for the money— $4.17. It comprised table-service for three, and kitchen-utensils, all of agate-ware, packed in an agate-ware bucket and secured by a strap, so that the whole outfit could be fastened on the back of a pack-mule or carried by a single man. Having the cooking-utensils, the next thing was to get a cook. There was a time when it was easy to find in an average troop or company of colored soldiers as many men able and willing to cook as one could wish, but such is not always the case now. This may be due to the "advancement" of the colored race, or to our colored troops being recruited more in the North and less in the South, proportionately, than they were; or to the fact that of late years officers' servants have not been exempt from drill and other duties; or, finally, to the cause, whatever it may be, of the general scarcity of good cooks outside of the army. In the navy, men are enlisted as officers' servants; in the army, officers have to find servants as best they can. On the frontier it is often impossible, and, on account of the high scale of wages, commonly impracticable for officers to secure servants other than soldiers. I have experienced the advantage there of having a Chinaman or other civilian for a servant. When the troop is ordered into the field, there is no question as to his remaining in the post to look after and wait on my family. But, apart from that, I prefer, in garrison and in the field, soldiers to civilians as servants. I interviewed one of my men to engage him as a cook, but he had just had an experience as troop-cook, and did not want any more cooking for some time.

But there were others in the troop who could cook, and I felt sure I would be able to find one who would do so for our mess (my Second Lieutenant and myself). Of course I proposed to offer him the usual compensation for cooking for an officer—from five to ten dollars a month. But about this time I heard that our regiment was soon to move to Tampa, and, besides, that there were no commissary supplies in camp for sale to officers. Under these circumstances, Kennington and I decided to put off the starting of our mess until we should be established in our new camp. In the mean time we continued to mess with other officers.

For furniture I went to Chattanooga. After a deal of hunting I secured a rickety wire cot. I had intended to get a canvas one, which folds up so as to go on a pack-mule, but there was none of that pattern left. I bought two folding-chairs, a wash-basin, and small looking-glass. It seemed to me that as the government did not furnish these things, nor keep them for sale, it would pay dealers to keep a full stock of them, and even peddle them in the camp. As a mess could not very well be run without a table, and I could not find a regular mess-table, I bought a seamstress'-table, which was very light and shaky, but combined with the advantage of portability the convenience of a yard-measure, laid off in feet and inches.

CAMP THOMAS, GEORGIA

There was some talk among our officers of forming a regimental mess, as cheaper and more sociable than troop messes; but the scheme was argued down, principally on the ground that a regimental mess would necessarily break up the troop messes, and that this would result in great inconvenience in case of troops being detached or the regiment split up.

From no quartermaster in camp could I buy a campaign hat, or pair of gauntlets, or riding-leggings. For these articles I sent to a firm in New York. Several weeks passed before I received them. In the mean time I wore a borrowed hat and gauntlets, and the abominable regulation riding-boot. There was no uniformity in what the officers wore on their feet. Some wore boots, some leggings, and some shoes with boot-tops (cut off old boots) in lieu of leggings. The boots and leggings were of various kinds—some high, some low, some black, some tan. Some of the leggings were of canvas and some of leather. The best riding-boot that I know of is the Thompson boot. It laces over the instep, and is therefore always easy to put on or take off. I think it better for cavalry than any legging. Among the articles of an officer's equipment which I had to provide myself with was a saddle-cloth. This is an ornamental covering for the blanket which goes under the saddle. I never could see any use in it, and wish it were abolished. It is an unneces-

sary weight for the horse, and adds to the con-
spicuousness of an officer, which is already greater
than it should be. With straps on his shoulders
and stripes on his legs, an officer is sure, indeed, to
catch bullets wherever he goes. During the campaign of Santiago many of our officers wore the
garrison blouse, which is distinguished from the
blouse of the men by the absence of buttons as
well as by the presence of shoulder-straps, a stand-
ing-collar, and insignia on the collar. The campaign blouse was not adopted until after the war
commenced. It has a turn-down instead of a
standing collar, outside instead of inside pockets,
and brass buttons. I can see no reason why it
should not replace the old blouse in garrison. It
does not seem to me that an officer should have
to buy a new style uniform to go to war in,
especially after war is declared. It is a striking
commentary on the dearth of field-exercises in
our army that a declaration of war finds our
officers without a uniform altogether suitable to
wear in time of war, at any season, in any climate.
Yet every few years since I came into the army
I have had to buy a new uniform, in whole or in
part, to conform to a change prescribed by the
War Department. Since the Civil War, or in the
last thirty-two years, we have made but two
changes of drill regulations; I shall not attempt
to state the number of changes that have been
made in our uniform. Any one interested in the

question will find the subject treated up to a recent date in a large book with colored illustrations, published by the Quartermaster's Department. For the evolution of our drill regulations, I do not know of any official document to refer him to. It would seem that our general staff has had less time for thinking about tactics than for pondering on what Von Moltke called the "millinery of the military profession." I might with red tape and plenty of time have procured my saddle-cloth from the Ordnance Department, but I preferred to save both by dealing with a private firm, and I did.

The daily papers, which were hawked through the camp early and often, were read with avidity by officers and men. One morning I was startled by a loud and prolonged cheering. Looking in the direction from which it came, I could see men out in the company streets, waving their hats, and newspaper boys running from company to company, and each organization after another taking up the demonstration, which passed down the line to our camp and on through the infantry camps beyond. It was the rejoicing over Dewey's great victory at Manila. I was already impressed by the fact that the navy was making a better showing in the war than the army. The navy had a general staff school, and had worked out plans of mobilization in advance. The army had no general staff school. Brigades, divisions, and army corps were organized and placed in camps; and instead of being trained and sent to the front as units, were trained by companies and sent to the front as regiments. When a brigade or division was wanted for Cuba, Puerto Rico, or the Philippines, it was formed by taking a regiment here and a regiment there. Whatever may have been gained by this mode of procedure, *esprit de corps* was not. The navy had the great advantage of not having to be materially expanded for the war. Apart from the auxiliary navy, there were no volunteer or amateur naval commanders. The question of mobilization was a comparatively simple one, and the direction of operations was in the hands of experts. The government will doubtless take good care that our costly battle-ships are not left to the handling of militia or volunteer captains, but it thinks nothing of intrusting the lives of hundreds and thousands of soldiers to the veriest tyros in land warfare. Finally, the navy had an advantage over the army in its warrant-officers, a grade between that of commissioned officers and petty officers. The latter correspond to our non-commissioned officers. Warrant-officers are trained for their work by a course at the school for apprentices. The army has no grade like that of warrant-officer, and no such school as that for naval apprentices for its non-commissioned officers. The navy was in a better state of training than the army.

We were all eager for intimations regarding the movement of troops, especially in the direction of Tampa. Officers were on the alert for reports of promotions. Our Colonel, Guy V. Henry, was the first, if I remember rightly, to be promoted out of our regiment. He was made a Brigadier-General of Volunteers. Other officers of the regiment were offered staff positions in the Volunteers. Some accepted and some declined. While not absolutely decided, I was strongly inclined to decline any promotion that would take me out of the regular establishment, especially as I was in a colored regiment. I felt that the colored troops were sure to go to the front, and active service was what I wanted. I preferred a captaincy in Cuba to a colonelcy in Georgia or Florida or anywhere else. I felt, too, that during the early part of the war, and throughout the war, if it were a short one, which I expected, the Volunteers would not do or see as much fighting as the Regulars; that the Regulars would habitually be at the front in advancing and at the rear in retreating—in short, where it was most interesting; and that the colored troops would probably be among the first to enter and the last to leave the theatre of active operations. For over twenty years I had labored under the disadvantage of serving in a colored regiment. I was now in a position to derive some advantage from it, and was quite set on doing so. My subsequent experience, however, proved that I was borrowing trouble in apprehending danger of a transfer from the colored troops by promotion.

I heard that the Colonel of a white regiment requested or suggested that the colored troops be removed from the camp, as their presence was degrading or humiliating to the others. Regarding the relations of the people hereabouts with our men, the following story was current in the regiment. One of the men, going into a barroom in Chattanooga, was refused a drink on account of his color. As he started to go out, the barkeeper followed him, remarking: "I don't see what they put you damned niggers in the army for, anyhow—you won't fight." At that the colored soldier turned around and hit this nigger-hater between the eyes, laying him out on his back. One or two assistant barkeepers rushed to assist their chief, but the soldier now proved himself as active with his legs as he had been with his fists, and was out of the door and around the corner before they could reach him.

Several batches of recruits came to us at Camp Thomas, mostly without any clothing but what they had on their backs. I procured furloughs for several of my recruits to enable them to go to their homes for underclothing. The Quartermaster's Department could not supply the wants of the men in the companies, to say nothing of the recruits.

The officers were puzzled and vexed at the dilution of the Regular regiments with recruits. Expecting to enter upon a campaign in a few days or weeks, they believed the recruits would prove a weakness rather than a strength to the army. If the campaign was not to commence until the fall, they could not see why the recruits should be sent to the regiments. They might have been better drilled in army posts, where there were riding-halls, fencing outfits, targets, and target-ranges, than they could at Camp Thomas, where there were none of these appointments. Each regiment should have had a depot at an army post from which recruits should have been forwarded as fast as they were trained and equipped, and no faster—until the regiment was brought up to its legal strength. After that they should have been forwarded on requisition of the regimental commander to repair losses. In the German army such requisition is made when the loss amounts to ten per cent.

In the course of the war our Volunteers experienced even greater embarrassments and discomforts in their camps in the United States than did the Regulars. This may be attributed in the main to the disregard by the War Department of General Miles's recommendation that not more than about 162,000 men should be mobilized at the beginning of the war, the Volunteers to remain in State camps until equipped and trained for field-service. [See report of Secretary of War, 1898, pp. 20, 22.]

III

BY RAIL TO LAKELAND, FLORIDA

WHEN rumors commenced flying through the camp that certain regiments were ordered farther south, the Tenth Cavalry pricked up its ears to catch a report of its being one of them. It was soon gratified. On the 10th of May it heard that it was going to New Orleans, and on the 11th that it was going to Tampa. Most of the officers and men were highly elated, notwithstanding that many had to part with wives and sweethearts, who had followed them to the vicinity of the camp or resided there. The only exception that I heard of was a short, chubby, jet-black recruit of my troop, who remarked: "I don't like dis goin' to Florida. I'se 'fraid I'll get sunburnt."

Clothing was issued to the troops on the 11th. Every soldier has a money allowance for clothing which he can draw on pretty much as he pleases. What he saves by not drawing his full allowance is paid to him on his discharge. What he draws in excess of his allowance is charged against his pay. His clothing account is kept by his company commander, but in his

"soldier's pocket-book," furnished by the government, he should always have a memorandum
of how his clothing account stands. It is the
exception rather than the rule for the Quartermaster's Department to *fill* a requisition for
clothing. There is always something lacking.
On this occasion there were no shoes, no under-
shirts, and only one size of hats, $7\frac{3}{8}$, which was
too large for most of my men. The trousers
gave out before the issuing was half done. I
succeeded in getting a pair of leggings for myself by having a soldier who did not want them
draw a pair and sell them to me.

The plan for "entraining" the command was
announced on the evening of the 13th. I was
given charge of a section to consist of thirteen
stock-cars, one baggage-car, and one passenger-
coach. The stock-cars were for the horses of
the first squadron — I belonged to the third
squadron; the baggage-car for the forage for the
two hundred and forty-seven horses of the first
squadron, and the equipments of my troop; the
passenger-coach for forty-five men and two
officers of my troop. All the horses and about
fifteen men of my troop were assigned to another section. For transportation to the railroad my troop was allowed three six-mule
wagons. One of them was packed after dark
on the 13th, and the other two on the following
morning. Reveille was sounded on the 14th, at

three o'clock. After we had finished packing we had to clean up the ground for the next encampment. Even the picket-posts had to be taken up and the ground left as if no camp had been there.

It was 10.30 when the band struck up and we started on the march for the station of Rossville. We arrived there about noon. While awaiting the arrival of our wagons, the officers and men scurried about buying something to eat at booths, stands, wagons, etc. I got two ham sandwiches to last me until evening, when I expected to eat supper at another station. The officers were expected to subsist themselves in this way. For the men I had travel-rations —canned beef, canned beans, hard bread, and money to buy sweetened coffee with.

The loading, especially of the horses, was attended with the confusion to be expected in the absence of a general staff-officer, or other official competent to control both the troops and the railroad. The trouble in moving troops by rail in our country arises chiefly from the ignorance of railroad men in military matters and of military men in railroad matters. Horses were put into cars with their heads where their tails ought to have been, but the railroad people did not care, so the cars were loaded and the train moved out. I heard that they tried to get the regiment off with one car less than the contract called for, but the regimental commander properly insisted on having that car, though it should go empty.

After repeated counting by Lieutenant Kennington, First Sergeant Givens, and myself, I got exactly forty-five of my men seated in the coach assigned to me, and saw to its provisioning with travel-rations. There being no ice in the water-tank, I got a piece from a store near the station, for which the proprietor refused payment. This was the only case of my getting anything to eat or drink from a civilian during the war without having to pay for it. Ahead of me was a section similar to mine, under Captain Reade, and in rear of me another, under Captain Hunt. In addition to these three sections, carrying the horses and most of the men of the three squadrons, there was a section for the band and headquarters, and one for the wagons, making altogether five sections.

About half-past two o'clock, amid handshaking and waving of handkerchiefs, with cries of " Good-bye !" and " Take care of yourself !" ringing in our ears, we started, and rolled off on the steel highway to Florida. Kennington and I occupied the smoker. Having been packing, marching, and loading since three o'clock in the morning, we enjoyed our cushioned seats, and being bowled along at the rate of from twenty-five to thirty miles an hour. Our route lay parallel to that followed by Sherman in his march to Atlanta, and presented substantially the appearance of his theatre of operation. We expected to reach Tampa about 4.15 P.M. the following day.

We reached Atlanta in the middle of the night, and spent about two hours and a half in watering and feeding the horses. The forage was taken out of the baggage-car, hoisted to the top of it, distributed along the tops to the several stock-cars, and fed to the animals through openings which we had some difficulty in finding and working. The water was fed by a hose from a hydrant into troughs running along both sides of each car on the inside. The horses were first watered in these troughs through the grating forming the sides of the cars. They were then fed grain in them. As some of the horses faced one way and some the other, they had dropped more or less dung in the troughs on each side of the cars. The troughs were designed to be emptied by turning them over, but the mechanism by which this was to be done would not work, and as a consequence the horses had to be watered with dung and water, which most of them sniffed at and would not drink.

Kennington and I got our supper about two o'clock the following morning, and our breakfast about ten o'clock. We had partaken of the coffee furnished the troop for breakfast. This portion of the ration was procured by telegraphing ahead for it. The parties who provided it, realizing that they had a monopoly of the business, tried to cheat us out of our sugar, and palmed off some pretty sloppy stuff on us. Troops travelling by rail would fare better and cheaper if they made their own coffee.

We stopped again for watering and feeding the horses, from about 10 A.M. to 12.30 P.M. We had lost time, and did not expect to reach Tampa until about 9 P.M. The country was growing flatter and more uninteresting. There was not a sleeper in the car, so we were all pretty tired. At the stations there were usually crowds of idle-looking people, mostly colored, to stare at us. Here and there they waved their hats. During the French and German War of 1870–72, being in Germany, I saw the German troops, going by rail to the Rhine, supplied at the stations with beer, sausages, and cigars by the people. In my journey from Georgia to Florida I did not see so much as a crust of bread thrown at a soldier. But apart from a little discomfort due to the irregularity with which they got their coffee, my men did not suffer, and they enjoyed the rapid change of scene and of society. For my part I found little pleasure in the sight or conversation of the people whom I passed. But I was cheered by the present of a bouquet handed me by a young lady, whose name and address I found concealed within it. The sequel of this incident I need not tell further than to state that I tried in

a letter to acknowledge my obligations and describe the feelings which the graceful compliment
had awakened in me.

This evening (May 15th) my section caught up
with Captain Reade's at a station where both sections remained long enough for Captain Reade
and myself to take supper at a restaurant. We
heard it rumored here that our destination had
been changed, as it had been found at Tampa
that there was no suitable camping-ground there
for the Tenth Cavalry. We realized that we
were absolutely in the power of the railroad company. All that we had to do, and it was more
than I succeeded in doing, was to keep our men
from being left on the road. I lost two or three
of my men, who were picked up by the section
in rear of mine. When we started again we understood that we were going by a branch road to
our new destination, but where this was, or when
we were to reach it, we could not guess. I expected to be enlightened on these points by telegraph,
but I was not. When I woke up, at five o'clock
the following morning, I found my section without an engine — side-tracked at a place which
proved to be Lakeland, Florida. I sent my
Lieutenant up to the station, about eight hundred
yards off, to see if we could get coffee there,
and he found that we could. I got out of the
car and walked up and down, thinking that some
one at the station would bring me a telegram, or

that some superior officer would turn up to tell me what to do with my men and horses—but nothing of the kind happened. I found that Captain Reade's and Captain Hunt's sections were at the station, in exactly the predicament of mine. Captain Hunt being the senior officer present, I suggested to him to take charge of things. We went together to the office of the station-agent to see if we could find any information there as to what we should do. The station-agent knew nothing about it; but while we were in his office he received a telegram for the commanding officer of the First Cavalry, which read :

"The brigade commander directs me to inform you that the destination of the brigade has been changed to Lakeland, forty-one miles east of Tampa. Act accordingly."

On the strength of this communication we proceeded to unload. We tied our horses to bushes and trees, and to improvised picket-ropes, formed of doubled lariats,* and sat about in such shade as we could find, to wait for the brigade commander or some other superior officer to come along and tell us where to camp. We

---

* A lariat is a light rope about thirty feet long with a picket-pin fastened to one end of it, which a cavalryman carries on his saddle. In using it regularly, the picket-pin is driven into the ground and the other end secured to the horse's halter.

34

understood that the First Cavalry and Sixth Ohio Cavalry were brigaded with our regiment. The First Cavalry arrived before the headquarters of the Tenth, having been sandwiched in between the parts of the Tenth. The brigade commander arrived in the course of the afternoon and assigned the regiments to their camp-ground. Portions of our regiment which did not arrive until late could not get to camp until the following day (May 17th).

Many of the men went to bed hungry in consequence of the wagons not having come up from the railroad to the camp. The work of getting the wagons off the truck-cars, and hitched up and in motion, was carried on until late at night. The teamsters had difficulty in handling the green mules which many of their teams were composed of. In consequence of this difficulty, and the darkness of the night, several wagons were abandoned on the way to the camp, which was not half a mile from the station. These wagons were found in the morning, sunk in sand or ruts, or caught on stumps or in bushes close to their destinations.

IV

IN CAMP AT LAKELAND

ONE of our men tried to buy a drink of soda-water in town, and was told: "We don't sell anything to damned niggers." An altercation ensued, in which the soldier drew his pistol and killed an unoffending by-stander. This incident gave the regiment a bad name, and occasioned many reports about it which were utterly without foundation. But little by little the people learned by observation that the colored troops were not on the whole any worse citizens than the white, and that they were just as good customers. They commenced to treat them accordingly, and there was no further trouble on the color line.

The people of the South did not seem to realize what military training does for a negro. They knew the negro as a slave, as a menial servant, and as a vagrant, criminal, and pauper, but they did not seem to know him as a soldier. They could not believe that he had any fight in him. The gallantry of the colored troops at Las Guasimas and Santiago have doubtless opened their eyes to the truth on this point, and increased the self-respect and stimulated the aspirations of the colored race. If our Southern brethern would treat colored soldiers with decent civility, however much they might discriminate against them, they would have little trouble with them. But these proud Caucasians, it seems, cannot find it in themselves to say: "We do not deal with colored people"; they have to say: "We don't sell anything to damned niggers." Many of our colored soldiers are born and bred in the North, and are quite unused to such language. It is hardly to be wondered at if, having the means to do so, they resent the insult by forever stopping the mouth from which it issues. The officers of the colored regiments are not surprised at the way their men behaved in battle. They knew that the colored troops would do their duty. Had they not seen them, in Indian campaigns, march and fight, go hungry and thirsty, and as scouts and guides carry their lives in their hands across weird, silent wastes of curling grass and chaparral, through gloomy, resounding cañons, and over wild crags and mountain-tops, as if they did not know what fear was?

I heard this morning (May 16th) that Sampson's fleet had met Cervera's, that it destroyed seven of the enemy's vessels, and that our *Indiana* and *New York* were blown up; also that our diversion from the route to Tampa was due to the fact that certain colored soldiers at Tampa, being refused liquor at a bar, had behaved in a disorderly manner, and that pressure had consequently been brought to bear upon the War Department to prevent more colored troops being sent there.

Our camp was on a lake, called Wire Lake, about a mile in circumference. We were in a pine wood. The trees were tall, and not very close together, and their branches very high and rather bare. We had not much shade, but it was well that we had not. The trees rested the eye without causing or harboring any miasma. The ground was sandy, which was unfavorable for drilling but easy for digging. The camp of the First Cavalry was on a similar site on the opposite side of the railroad from the Tenth, about a mile from it. These two regiments of the brigade remained thus separately encamped until they moved to Tampa about three weeks later. The instruction of the regiments was not materially different from what it had been at Chickamauga. We commenced our drilling with three hours a day — troop, from 7.30 to 9 A.M., and squadron, from 3 to 4.30 P.M. The time was afterwards reduced to an hour and a half a day (7 to 8.30 A.M.), and devoted to troop-drill. The change in the time and duration of the drill was ordered from division or corps headquarters on account of the heat. I thought this a singular measure in our preparation for a campaign which might involve marching and fighting at all hours of the day and night through a tropical summer. But far be it from me to criticise. I wish only to record that the philosophy, or rationale, of our training at this time was too deep for me.

As to brigade instruction, there was none. The regiments were not united for a single parade, review, drill, inspection, field-exercise, or anything else. During most, if not all, of our stay near Lakeland, the brigade commander had his headquarters in a hotel in town. His regiments were never formed in the same line of battle until they came under the fire of Spanish rifles. It is hardly necessary to add that there was no division exercise. The division commander visited the camps once. He did not have the regiments united or mounted. His inspection of the Tenth Cavalry consisted in walking through the company streets dismounted, and interviewing the officers. This was the only inspection made of our regiment during the campaign, except by officers of the regiment. I do not remember seeing an officer of the Inspector-General's Corps inspecting anything.

We kept on receiving recruits, arms, clothing, etc., and having them doled out to us in driblets; we were continually making out vouchers for inadequate supplies. I understood that the army as a whole fared the same way; that no

corps was selected to be recruited up and supplied, commencing with one regiment, going from
that regiment to the other regiments of the same
brigade, from that brigade to the other brigades
of the same division, and then to the other divisions. There was too much uncertainty, it seems,
as to which regiments would win in the scramble
for service in Cuba.

Each fresh accession of recruits formed a new
class for which additional instructors had to be
detailed and separate instruction prescribed. If
I had gotten all my recruits in one batch, they
could have been carried along and put into the
troop together. This would have necessitated a
comparatively large force of instructors for a time,
but it would not have kept the instructors so long
from the troop as the small and changing force
was kept by the method—if it may be so called—
which actually obtained, and it would not have
wearied the commissioned and non-commissioned
officers nearly so much. Many of the recruit-
drills took place at the same hour as the troop
and squadron drills, being conducted by non-
commissioned officers, without even the super-
vision of commissioned officers. I got permission
from the regimental commander to excuse my
Lieutenant from all other drill in order that he
might attend recruit-drill. There was a great
deal of time lost through the incompetency of
our non-commissioned officers as drill-masters.

I observed them in my own troop and in other troops of the regiment. I could hardly watch a squad half a minute without seeing faults which the instructor did not correct. I am of the opinion that recruits should be received in large batches at long intervals, and that all officers available should assist in their instruction. During the period of recruit-drill, the troop and squadron drills might be suspended altogether, or conducted by non-commissioned officers not needed for recruit-drill. Trained soldiers can do without officers better than recruits.

The Sixth Ohio Cavalry, if there was such a regiment, did not come to Lakeland. We were joined, however, by the Seventy-first New York and the Second Massachusetts. The men looked, and doubtless were, younger than the Regulars. They were of lighter weight, and comparatively pale looking. They took hold of their drill with a will, and I believe attained a high degree of proficiency in it, but they did not seem to know or learn much about laying out and taking care of a camp. When I rode through their camps I was struck by the closeness of the tents to one another, the company streets seemed narrow, and the officers' tents not far enough from the men's. In every direction I saw old newspapers, tin cans, cast-off clothing, and other rubbish. It is hardly an exaggeration to say that there was more dirt in one of their company streets than in our whole camp. I understand that the commanding officers of these regiments were allowed to choose the sites for their camps. If that was the case, they might perhaps have done well to have fixed their choice upon points close to the camps of the Regulars, which would have served as object-lessons to them.

Out of regard for the chaste sensibilities of the people of Lakeland, no bathing in Wire Lake was allowed during the day. The hour for bathing was first from 8 to 10 P.M., and afterwards from 8 to 9 P.M. I resorted to an ice factory in town, where I got a shower-bath of tepid water under a common spigot for ten cents, and a drink of ice-water for nothing.

Little by little I learned how to make myself as comfortable as possible in a Southern climate. When I first came South, I suffered occasionally from an oppression in the head. I thought at one time that I must have had a touch of sun-stroke. After cutting a hole about half an inch square in each side of my hat, I had no further trouble of the kind. I recommended my remedy to the troop, and observed that most of the men adopted it. When, a few weeks later, I felt the searching force of a tropical rain, I appreciated the fact that many of my men had improved on my method by cutting only three sides of the opening, leaving a flap with which to close it. I left off my undershirt and wore only a linen shirt

42

under my blouse. The latter was of light India serge, but I made it lighter by cutting out the lining. I learned, too, the advantage, in point of coolness, of sleeping without a pillow.

The press censorship was so strict that we received very little news. As at Camp Thomas, our chief topic of conversation was the prospect of a move. Next to that came perhaps the latest promotions.

To make ourselves as independent as possible of the town, we established a canteen, at which lemonade, soda-water, and novelties were kept for sale. At first it was decided not to keep beer, but this decision was afterwards reversed, and the consequences were generally satisfactory.

V

TO TAMPA BAY AND EMBARKATION

ON the 29th of May I read in my newspaper that all the cavalry (about nine thousand) was to be concentrated at Lakeland under the command of General Wheeler. On the evening of the 30th, Lieutenant Smith (killed, a month later, at San Juan) started with twenty-five men of my troop and about an equal number of his own to march to Tampa and bring back a batch of about one hundred and fifty horses. We received about that number of recruits the day before. General Miles was reported to have gone to Tampa, which looked like a move to Cuba, but our horses and recruits coming to Lakeland did not. It was hard to form any idea of what we were going to do. The skeleton troops (L and M) were being manned, and I was asked by the regimental commander whether I wished to take troop M, to which I had nominally belonged, or to retain troop D, which I actually commanded. I chose to retain troop D. Within a day or two our first squadron was ordered to hold itself in readiness to move without its horses. I assumed that it was to go soon to Cuba. On the 2d of June our second squadron received similar orders. This squadron, which had numbered but three troops, was increased by the addition of my troop (D). The band and headquarters were afterwards added to this force, which thus became the main body of the regiment, or regiment proper. The other four troops formed a squadron, to remain behind with the horses and extra baggage. I prepared my troop in accordance with the following detailed instructions:

MEMORANDUM

Will at once prepare to take the field and stand ready to march when ordered. Squadron will be dismounted and composed of trained men only, the horses being turned over to the remaining squadron. Will be equipped with five hundred rounds of carbine ammunition per man. Revolvers and sabres will not be taken, except one revolver by sergeants.

Requisitions for haversacks will be submitted by each troop at once.

Respectfully,

—— ——, Major Tenth Cavalry,

Commanding Second Squadron.

June 2, 1898.

In the course of the next few days our saddles and everything else that was to be left behind were packed up. We still had the horses to groom and feed but not to ride. It was rather a damper on our ardor for active service

45

that we had to part with our horses. Many of us had been studying and experimenting for twenty years and more to learn how we should care for our horses and handle ourselves as cavalry in the presence of an enemy. We were now about to meet a real enemy, and by a stroke of the pen were converted into infantry. We heard that General Miles had stated that our horses would be sent after us. But we doubted whether the General, if he had made such a statement, would be able to make it good. We did not expect to see our horses again during the campaign, and we did not. I had just finished paying, by instalments, $125 for an indifferent animal, which I had bought in Chattanooga, to carry me along the wretched roads of Cuba and into the ranks of the Spanish cavalry. The new, dismounted, squadron to which I belonged had one drill before we left Lakeland, and none afterwards. Our skirmish-drills are generally too rigid. There is too much attention given to the intervals between the men, and not enough to their positions as to cover for their bodies and rests for their pieces, their estimation of distances, the elevations actually taken, etc. About half of the men in my troop had never had any target-practice; the rest were good shots. A similar state of things obtained throughout the provisional regiment of eight troops which was to go to Cuba. I felt that if the military problem were a simple one—a direct front attack or a passive defence—the regiment would render a good account of itself; but if the problem involved considerable manœuvring, or splitting up and co-operation in a number of columns, or re-forming after a repulse, it would make a poor showing. From lack of field-exercises, it was not used to facing the unexpected, which is the usual thing in war. But the men were in good health and spirits, their physique excellent, and they had unbounded confidence in their officers.

On the 6th we were ordered to put our baggage (rations, tentage, etc.) on the cars, and told that the men would be entrained in the evening, and would spend the night in the cars. About 7.30 P.M. I was informed that the train would not be ready for the men until the following morning, and that the troops would bivouac in their old camp. By this time all my property had been loaded. My men slept in their shelter-tents. Kennington and I slept in officers' tents which were to remain up or had not yet been taken down. We had no means of cooking breakfast. I had not even kept a towel out for myself. Reveille was to be sounded on the 7th at about half-past 3 A.M., and the troops to be ready to get on the train at half-past four. By mistake the Colonel had reveille sounded at half-past two. My men breakfasted with one of the troops that remained behind. After breakfast they sat

around and smoked and "chinned" until time
had dragged itself on to the point when they
were to fall in for the last time by Wire Lake.
With the band playing, the troops broke in succession from the right in columns of twos, and
marched past the remaining troops to the left,
out of the camp, along the border of the lake,
and through the straggling outskirts of Lakeland
to the station. This was the first time that I saw
my regiment carrying their blankets and shelter-
tents in rolls (*en bandoulière*) like infantrymen.
There was something grotesque in it to my cavalry eye. On arriving at the station we remained
standing for about half an hour, in the course of
which it transpired that the train was not ready
for us. Shortly after we had halted, the Colonel,
observing that my Lieutenant and myself did not
have our sabres on, inquired of me where they were,
and on learning that they were in camp, ordered
me to get them or send for them. A sabre is an
awkward thing to carry dismounted. According
to the drill regulations, when cavalry dismounts
to fight on foot, the officers, like the men, leave
their sabres attached to the saddles, unless otherwise directed. I had not been otherwise directed, and considered myself a dismounted cavalryman.

To wait for the train, our regiment was marched
into an enclosúre in the main square of the town,
near the station, and there remained in the broil-

ing sun until afternoon—altogether about seven
hours. The men were allowed, a few at a time,
to go out to a store or restaurant near by.
Fortunately they had been paid not long before,
and many of them had money. There was no
lunch to give them except hard bread. I was
going to have some issued, but the First Sergeant told me that the men would not eat it.
They would prefer waiting, he said, until we got
to Tampa, and could have a square meal. So I
made the mistake of not giving them what food
I had. I left all the hard bread in the baggage-
car. We should have had canned meat. Why
we did not I do not know, unless it was that our
brigade commissary was a Volunteer officer fresh
from civil life. However that may have been,
this officer proved himself alive to his respon-
sibilities, and fitted himself to fulfil their highest
requirements. He was wounded at San Juan
while attending to the distribution of rations on
the firing-line.

Most of the officers took lunch at a hotel.
At eleven o'clock we were about to get on the
train, when the Colonel, having inspected the
cars and discovered that there was no ice in the
water-coolers, delayed the operation until the
railroad company had repaired that little omission. We boarded the train between 11.45 and
12, and started at 12.38. We reached Tampa Bay
about 3 P.M., and disembarked on the pier, fac-

ing a line of steam-transports about a mile long. A march of a few hundred yards through a crowd of civilians and soldiers brought us to the *Leona* (No. 21), and we proceeded to embark. The Major of the second squadron, to which I belonged, led me in pitchy darkness through a maze of improvised bunks, four in a tier, between decks, in the after-part of the vessel. After I had groped my way out I took my troop and led it in single-file into this black hole. To make sure that the men were accommodated, I had each one get into a bunk. The bunks were made of undressed lumber, and consisted of planks to lie on, with a rim about six inches high all around. In this place the occupant kept all his effects, including his carbine and ammunition. There were no gun-racks on board. After the men were assigned to their quarters I wanted to give my men some supper, and found that there was nothing whatever to give them. The cars containing our rations were several miles behind, and the intervening railroad completely blocked. I went to a restaurant on the pier to make arrangements to have the men eat there, and was told by the lady who kept it that to have colored men eat in her dining-room would ruin her business. After making all possible inquiries, and ineffectually trying every place within reach, I returned to the transport, and sadly told First Sergeant Givens that I felt for the men, but could not do anything to relieve their hunger. Excepting the coffee and hard bread they ate about three o'clock in the morning, they had not received anything to eat from the Government since the night before. To my surprise, Sergeant Givens informed me that the men had gotten something to eat by buying it, and that he did not believe any of them could be very hungry. I suppose they bought fruit, cakes, pies, and sandwiches from peddlers along the pier.

Loud and deep was the profanity with which the sound of reveille was greeted the following morning at four o'clock. Without breakfast, the men were put to work taking the baggage off the cars and loading it on the transport. I was told by my squadron commander to put my baggage on where my men went on, and pile it where they were quartered. When I had gotten about half of it aboard and deposited as directed, I was told by the regimental Quartermaster that all the baggage should be put in the hold in the forward part of the vessel. In view of these conflicting instructions, I went to the regimental commander and asked him whose instructions I should follow, the Major's or the Quartermaster's, and was told to follow the Quartermaster's. I had accordingly to get my men to take off the part of the baggage which they had put aboard, and carry all our baggage forward and place it in the hold. The First Cavalry and headquarters, which had followed us from Lakeland, went aboard, men and baggage, about the same time as we did. The confusion which characterized the work of putting the stores and baggage of the sixteen troops, two bands, and brigade headquarters aboard and into the hold, I shall not attempt to describe. No one seemed to be in charge. The troop commanders asked any and everybody to tell them where to put their things. I was asked by staff-officers and others, among whom was Major-General Miles, commanding the army, if I knew when the loading of our transport would be completed. I answered that, according to the best of my judgment, it would be in about two hours, and observed that my answer did not seem to please the General. There was no partition of the space in the hold. Each organization put its sacks of bacon, beans, rice, sugar, tent-pins, its rolls of tents, bundles of picks, shovels, axes, etc., all together in as orderly a heap as possible, immediately adjoining that of another organization. The property of some of the organizations was covered by that of others. I saw sacks of flour and other packages burst open on the bottom of the hold and on the top of the heap, and heard the trickling of rice, beans, and coffee from broken packages into and through the heap. After I had gotten the property of my troop stowed away, I reported the fact to my regimental commander, and was told that I should not eat my breakfast until all the property of the regiment was aboard. There was no breakfast - call. I gave my men breakfast as soon as it could be gotten ready, which was at half-past six, about thirty-six hours after the last square meal furnished them by the Government. This morning, our travel-rations (coffee, hard bread, sugar, salt, canned beef, canned beans, and canned tomatoes) were issued to us. These were to be kept between decks where the men slept and ate. But in the excitement of getting things aboard, a material portion of my canned beef was spirited away ; possibly it was mixed up by mistake with the supplies of some other troop—and consumed before it was noticed—possibly it went with my tentage into the hold.* While our transport was

* It would be interesting in this connection to know what answer, if any, was made to the following communication :

IN THE FIELD, TAMPA, Florida, *June* 11, 1898.

SIR, — Please ascertain whether the following has been attended to in connection with your fleet of transports :

Have commanding officers required their transport officers to make a list of the contents of each ship, where stored, the bulk of such stores, and an estimate of how many wagon-loads there are in each vessel? Do the commanding officers of organizations know exactly where their supplies are? Have arrangements been made in order that if so many rations of any kind, ammunition, hospital supplies, etc., should be required, that they would know at once where they can be found? Have transports been supplied with stern-anchors to hold them in place and still tied up at the wharf, we were informed by a staff-officer on shore that Roosevelt's Rough Riders were brigaded with our regiment and the First Cavalry. Most of us had never seen the distinguished Volunteer regiment, to and with which we were henceforth to be organically related and more or less closely associated. A number of its officers and men, in their fresh and comfortable-looking khaki uniforms, were pointed out to me, and I wondered, as I looked at them, whether my men were really going to march and fight in the tropics in the uniforms which they had brought with them from Montana, and in which they had been sweltering in Georgia and Florida.

afford a lee for the landing of troops in case of necessity when sea is somewhat rough? What kind of small boats are supplied to each ship for the landing of the troops of that ship? Has a list been made of them and the total number of men they can safely land at one time? Have stores been put upon transports with a view that each organization's should be complete?

The great importance of these details cannot be overestimated. In landing, stores intended for one command are liable to be sent to another, and the necessity of having stores that may be needed accessible at once is manifest.

I would suggest that thorough attention be required to every detail in order to insure perfect order in the disembarking of your command. Respectfully yours,

MILES, Major-General Commanding.

General William R. Shafter,
Port Tampa, Florida.

VI

ON TRANSPORT IN TAMPA BAY

THIS morning, amid cheering and waving of handkerchiefs, we glided away from the wharf, past other transports in the process of loading, and, proceeding slowly a mile out in the bay, joined the transports that were riding at anchor with their passengers and cargoes aboard. A few gunboats seemed to stand guard over them. This afternoon many of our officers and men witnessed an occurrence which tended to shake their confidence in the sea-captains. A large transport was steaming slowly towards the wharf, heading for a point where a smaller, empty transport was moored. As the larger vessel approached the wharf it dropped anchor. The captain intended, I thought, to swing around towards the wharf, pivoting on his anchor. However that may have been, his vessel went dragging its anchor right on towards the wharf, and crashed into the smaller vessel square amidships. Men on the smaller vessel ran to the rail and looked over it at the other, which slowly extricated itself and withdrew, disclosing the huge

55

gash it had made. I looked to see the smaller vessel settle and go down or keel over, but happily it did not. The wound in her side did not extend to the water.

Most of the transports were passenger-vessels. They were commanded by their regular captains, all civilians. We had on the *Leona* a cadet in the first class at the Naval Academy, but his duty consisted chiefly in signalling, and in receiving and transmitting orders from the naval officers in charge of the fleet. The troops on board numbered about one thousand officers and men.* This afternoon one of the gunboats fired a few shots for practice. Each shot was greeted with cheers by the cavalry on the *Leona*. Our men rushed up the rigging or to the rail at the first indication of an interesting occurrence, and cheered at the slightest provocation, like a lot of small boys at a ball game. We expected to run down to the lower bay in the evening and go to sea in the morning; but before evening came, our instructions to go down the bay were revoked. There were various rumors as to the cause of the suspension of our operations. One was that a new Spanish fleet had turned up,

* The strength of the expedition is given by General Shafter, in his report, as 815 officers and 16,072 enlisted men. Lieutenant-Colonel Miley, General Shafter's chief of staff, gives it as 819 officers and 15,058 enlisted men. [*In Cuba with Shafter*, p. 44.]

another that peace proposals had been made, another that some of our transports were to unload for practice. None of our troops had practised the operation of landing from transports, and I thought it would be a good thing for us to do so, and to follow it up with a march of a few days' duration into the interior, bringing up our artillery (light and heavy), our medical stores, ambulances, etc., and deploying for the attack of a fortified place. We did not move from our anchorage until the following day, when with the other transports we went back to the wharf and tied up, while the gunboats took position farther down the bay. The men were sent ashore and taken on a march of about two miles for exercise. On the 10th we cast off, and again anchored out in the bay not far from the wharf, where we lay until the 13th.* On that day we moved a few miles down the bay and cast anchor again. It was the 14th, a week after our embarkation, when we finally started for the lower bay. During this long, tedious period of waiting we were governed in the main by the provisions

* Lieutenant-Colonel Miley, General Shafter's chief of staff, says in his book on the campaign (*In Cuba with Shafter*, p. 36): " Orders were given to the various commanding officers while lying in the channel to practise their men in disembarking and embarking." I saw no signs of any such orders being carried out by any commanding officer.

of the following order, published the day after our embarkation:

HEADQUARTERS SECOND CAVALRY BRIGADE,
ON BOARD U. S. TRANSPORT "LEONA,"
June 8, 1898.

The following instructions will be strictly complied with in this brigade during movements by water:

1. The top of the pilot-house and the starboard side of the upper deck of the ship aft of the pilot-house is reserved for officers. Enlisted men are given the freedom of the hurricane-deck and the port side of the upper deck to the after-deck. The guard will enforce this provision.

2. Troops will form at their bunks for inspection, without arms, by troop commanders, at 7 A.M. and 5 P.M. daily. Every individual will then be clean, his hands, face, and feet washed, and his hair combed. Troop commanders will also frequently inspect arms and accoutrements. Arms will be placed so as to be secure from injury, and ammunition-belts from fire.

3. Troop officers will enforce cleanliness about bunks, and will cause blankets to be taken daily on upper deck for airing, the same being replaced in bunks before sunset.

4. Smoking is prohibited between decks, nor will lights be permitted there except such ship-lanterns as the master of the transport may direct.

5. At the marine fire-alarm—a long, continuous whistle—the trumpeters of the guard will sound "fire-call." All enlisted men will promptly assemble at attention at their bunks, and officers will join their troops and there await orders. Staff-officers will immediately join their respective commanders. At the alarm "to arms" the same procedure will be observed.

6. During cooking-hours a troop officer of each troop will visit the galley and see that food is properly prepared.

7. Lights will be extinguished at "taps," when every enlisted man not on duty will be in his berth. The officer of the guard will see that this is enforced.

8. No officer will leave the ship without the permission of the Brigade Commander.

9. The Brigade Surgeon will make recommendations respecting the provisions of par. 165, "Troops in Campaign," * and such other matters as may be necessary for the health of the command.

10. Regimental commanders will prescribe occasional exercises for their commands so as to preserve their good health and condition.

By command, etc.

Though the inspections at 7 A.M. and 5 P.M. were ordered to be made by troop commanders (paragraph 2), I observed that the 7 A.M. inspection was usually made by a subaltern. These inspections were often the merest form, as the place in which they were made was dark as pitch. In case of an alarm of fire, or "to arms," the men being at their bunks (paragraph 5), it would have been rather awkward to get a troop or a squad together or in hand. But neither the "fire-call" nor the alarm "to arms" was sounded during the voyage, even for practice. Paragraph 6 was inoperative, as there was no cooking done, and therefore no galley used. The nearest approach to cooking was the use of boiling water in mak-

* Regulations for field-service.

ing coffee, the water being drawn in buckets from an apparatus connected with the boilers. Paragraph 7 was, I believe, a dead letter. So far as I know, the men had no lights to extinguish, the only lights below deck being those of the ship, which the men were not allowed to handle. The officers were not expected to put their lights out. On account of the heat the men were permitted to sleep on deck. Paragraph 10 proved ineffectual for lack of instructions assigning to either regiment the time or place in which it was to exercise, so that it should not interfere with the other regiment. This omission was remedied by the following order superseding the paragraph in question:

General Field Orders, No. 11.

> HEADQUARTERS SECOND CAVALRY BRIGADE,
> ON BOARD S. S. "LEONA,"
> TAMPA BAY, Florida, *June* 11, 1898.

*   *   *   *   *   *   *

While on shipboard, circumstances permitting, troops will be exercised daily on the saloon-deck in such of the setting-up exercises as can be practised. Regimental commanders will see that squadron commanders supervise the exercises of their squadrons.

The saloon-deck will be used for this purpose in accordance with the schedule given below.

Regimental commanders may cause squadron commanders to arrange for such rotation of troops of their squadrons as may seem advisable, and will cause troops to follow each other promptly, so that all time may be utilized.

First Squadron, Tenth Cavalry

11th	13th	14th	15th	16th	17th	18th
8 to 9.30 A.M.	9.30 to 11 A.M.	2 to 3.30 P.M.	3.30 to 5 P.M.	8 to 9.30 A.M.	9.30 to 11 A.M.	2 to 3.30 P.M.

First Squadron, First Cavalry

11th	13th	14th	15th	16th	17th	18th
9.30 to 11 A.M.	2 to 3.30 P.M.	3.30 to 5 P.M.	8 to 9.30 A.M.	9.30 to 11 A.M.	2 to 3.30 P.M.	3.30 to 5 P.M.

Second Squadron, Tenth Cavalry

11th	13th	14th	15th	16th	17th	18th
2 to 3.30 P.M.	3.30 to 5 P.M.	8 to 9.30 A.M.	9.30 to 11 A.M.	2 to 3.30 P.M.	3.30 to 5 P.M.	8 to 9.30 A.M.

Second Squadron, First Cavalry

11th	13th	14th	15th	16th	17th	18th
3.30 to 5 P.M.	8 to 9.30 A.M.	9.30 to 11 A.M.	2 to 3.30 P.M.	3.30 to 5 P.M.	8 to 9.30 A.M.	9.30 to 11 A.M.

By command, etc.

SANTIAGO CAMPAIGN

Three days after this order was published, one or two men fainted at the exercises, and there was no more regular exercise. The calls to duty were sounded as indicated in the following circular:

Circular }   HEADQUARTERS SECOND BRIGADE,
No. 7. }   ON BOARD S. S. "LEONA,"
TAMPA BAY, Florida, *June* 12, 1898.

The officer of the day will regulate the following instructions:

1. The trumpeter of the guard will sound, daily, first call for reveille at 4.45 A.M., when all trumpeters will assemble on deck. At 4.55 the march will be sounded, followed by reveille. No assembly.

2. First call for retreat will be sounded by the trumpeter of the guard at an hour so as to allow fifteen minutes between first call and the time of the assembly of the trumpeters and band, which will be at sunset. No formation will take place. The band of the First Cavalry will be used for the ceremony on the days of even dates, beginning to-day. The band of the Tenth Cavalry will be used on the days of uneven dates. Retreat will be sounded by the trumpeter, followed at the last note of the retreat by the band, which will play "The Star Spangled Banner." All officers and enlisted men standing will remove their hats, and quiet will be observed. At the last note of "The Star Spangled Banner" three cheers will be given.

3. First call for tattoo, 8.45 P.M. Tattoo by all the trumpeters at 9 P.M.

By command, etc.

I had never before known what it was to

cheer by order. Throughout the voyage the three cheers prescribed in paragraph 2 were given with a will by officers and men.

The men spent a good deal of their time in gambling. The portion of the deck allowed to them was thickly dotted, not to say covered, with card-parties. I had an outside state-room on the men's side of the ship, and could rarely get into it without stepping over a lay-out of poker, monte, crap, or some other game of chance. This state of things was abolished, and other matters of discipline regulated, by the following order:

Circular, }
No. 6. } HEADQUARTERS SECOND CAVALRY BRIGADE,
ON BOARD U. S. TRANSPORT "LEONA,"
June 11, 1898.

1. The attention of all officers of the brigade is called to the fact that owing to the restricted space aboard the ship and the close proximity of officers and men, there is no situation in which a stricter conformity to orders and regulations is more necessary for the welfare of the command than the present one. All officers should exercise the utmost vigilance that discipline is enforced and regularity and proper order maintained.

It is the duty of all to suppress at once any conduct or action prejudicial to good order in any way.

4. Gambling is forbidden in the brigade aboard the ship, and the officer of the day is responsible that none goes on.

5. The use of fresh water is prohibited except for cooking and drinking purposes. The officer of the day will enforce this by stationing a sentinel at each fresh-water receptacle with proper orders.

Troop commanders will caution their men against appearing without orders in that part of the ship already designated for the use of officers, and will forbid them spitting on the deck and over the side of the ship from the upper deck.

*   *   *   *   *   *   *

I was informed one morning by First Sergeant Givens that my troop was short of 193 pounds (nearly three days' rations) of canned beef.* The regimental commissary officer from whom I had my rations could find no evidence in his accounts of a shortage in his issues to me, and neither he nor the brigade commissary had any extra supplies. There seemed to be no reserve of anything in this campaign. As a general thing, if a man had a hole in his canteen he had to carry his drinking-water inside of him; if he lost a bolt or screw out of his gun, he had to use his gun as a club, so far as I could see. Our expedition of about twenty thousand men, going about one thousand miles from home, was equipped on the principles of a scouting-party. I congratulated myself on being notified of my shortage before the expedition started, and decided to make it good by purchase from the company fund. There was a steamer announced to stop at every transport every two hours, to take passengers and

* I have already referred to the loss of this beef as occurring during the loading of the transport.

packages ashore, but there was no hour stated for its arrival. After about an hour's waiting, I got aboard of it, taking with me five of my men, among whom was Sergeant Stratton, my Quartermaster - Sergeant. The boat had already stopped at a number of the transports, but going to the others, and from the last one to the shore, consumed two hours. I reached the shore about the time at which I had expected to be back on the transport. My first step was to call on the chief commissary officer of the expedition, who lived on a transport at the wharf. He told me that he had nothing to sell, that he only kept commissaries for issue, and, furthermore, that all the commissaries that he had were in a transport out in the harbor, giving me to understand that these would not be available, even for issue, until the expedition had landed in Cuba. He informed me that there were commissaries for sale at Tampa, about nine miles from Port Tampa by rail, and stated that trains were running between the two places at short intervals. I found on inquiry that there would not be a train for an hour and a half, or until about 4.45. At that hour I started off with my five men, whose fares, fifty cents apiece, I paid myself. At Tampa I found the commissary officer, and bought the canned beef. I also bought from a grocer's cans of fruit for the troop, enough for several messes. When I went to get on the train the baggage-master would not take my packages either as baggage or as freight. I had, therefore, to send them as express matter. But I went along with them in the express-car, and reached Tampa about 8 P.M. My men carried the packages to the landing, and there we learned, to our relief, that the boat which was to have left at 8 P.M. had not yet arrived. We settled down hopefully to wait for it. Nine and ten o'clock came, but no boat. In the mean time, a crowd of about one hundred officers and men had gathered at the landing to take passage to their transports. I went with a few other officers to a transport moored near by to wait for the ferry. About eleven o'clock it was seen coming. We all stirred ourselves, gathered up our packages, and stood ready to go aboard. The passengers on the boat went ashore, and then, to our consternation, the Captain announced that he was not going to make another trip. The crowd started in a body to vent its feelings, but some of the men calling out, " Be quiet, let the officers speak!" several officers expostulated in turn with the Captain, but with little effect, until an infantry officer from the transport on which I had been waiting got aboard of the ferry and spoke a few words in the Captain's ear. The landing-place was so cramped by two adjoining transports that the ferry could not get close enough to use a gang-plank. The stern of the

boat was brought in so that one could get aboard
by climbing up a cluster of piles and stepping
therefrom to the upper deck.   For a moment I
was afraid I would not get my packages aboard,
but my men proved equal to the occasion, and
we were soon gliding again in and out among the
transports.   As we approached each one in turn
our watch called out: "Whot noomber air ye?"
The answer being, say, "Twenty-five," the question was promptly and loudly asked all over the
boat: "Anybody for twenty-five?"   If there was
not, we did not stop, but there usually was.   I
was immensely relieved when (about 12.15 A.M.)
I climbed over the rail of the *Leona*, and saw my
detachment and our precious freight safely aboard
of her.

About 3.30 P.M. of the 12th, Troops C and F
of the second squadron of the Tenth Cavalry
were ordered to get ready to go to another transport, and were told that a boat would stop for
them in a few minutes.   They loaded themselves
with their rolls, canteens, etc., and waited.   Four
o'clock came, and no boat.   They went without
supper, expecting the boat every minute.   Seven
and eight o'clock, and still no boat.   About a
quarter of nine they were informed that they
would probably be called for in the morning.
At three o'clock in the morning they were turned
out and taken off.   Such occurrences tended to
shake our confidence in the officers who regu-

lated our movements and might hold our lives in their hands. The departure of two troops gave me a berth in a state-room opening into the saloon, with a window on deck. It was on the officers' side of the ship, and consequently much quieter than my former one.

I had not received a letter from home since leaving Lakeland. The post-offices between Tampa and Tampa Bay seemed to be swamped by the mail matter for and from the troops. In Germany, France, or Austria an army corps of thirty thousand men, halting for a night near the smallest hamlet, will have its mail distributed to it by the military postal corps. How much dejection and heartsickness might have been prevented among our troops by such an organization! Many a poor fellow who was never to return to his home or country was disappointed day after day in his expectation of a last parting message from father, mother, sister, or brother, or other dear one. Men could have been detailed, it would seem, from the army, to assist the regular postal corps to any extent that might be necessary, to sort and distribute the sacks of mail that were lying in the post-offices only a stone's-throw from some of the camps and transports. I understand that such a detail was actually made shortly before the expedition started —too late to accomplish its work.

The pleasantest feature of our life in and about

Port Tampa was the meeting of friends who had long been parted. When ashore, the meetings took place on the plank-walk, at the hotels, or on transports at their moorings. Out in the harbor two transports rarely passed each other without an interchange of greetings.

The transports, I understood, had steam up all the time, and cost the government on an average about one thousand dollars a day apiece. It seemed to me that they might occasionally run down the bay and back, or go around in a circle, to give us a little fresh air; but they did not. I am not finding fault. There may have been reasons why this could not, or should not, have been done; but none occurred to me, and it is just possible that there was none. While wishing to make all due allowances for the difficulties which officers had to contend against in creating and moving our field-army, I am not one of those who in answer to every criticism exclaim: "Oh, but you don't know what so-and-so knows, and the considerations which led him to do or not to do this or that." I suppose that if the crew of the *Leona* had been sent below with augurs to bore holes in the bottom of the ship, there would have been officers to say: "This is strange, but we do not know," etc.

VII

AT SEA

THE heat and spare diet had begun to tell on the men, when we finally started for the lower bay and had the benefit of a motion in the air due to the speed of about six miles an hour. The next week was spent in making our way at about this rate through the Bahama Channel and around the eastern end of Cuba to Santiago. Off the Florida Keys we were joined by the battle-ship *Indiana* and other war-vessels, which enveloped us with a cordon of security. I understood that the transports were to travel in two columns about half a mile apart, with an interval of about four hundred yards between vessels. I could hardly recognize this formation in our order of cruising. Now and then a despatch-boat would turn back to prod up some transport that was lagging behind, or to recall one that was straying out of the column. Occasionally a torpedo-boat or light cruiser would dart out to right or left, attracted by a trail of smoke or speck of canvas in the offing, and, upon examining it, circle back into position.

AT SEA

Among the crafts of the expedition were two large, low, flat‑bottomed scows, heavily decked over, to be used, I understood, in landing stores and artillery, and in the construction of a floating dock. One of these "lighters" was towed by the *Leona*. I noticed that the sole bond of connection between her and her tug was a single cable, and remarked to a brother officer that, if a storm should come up, that cable would snap and the lighter be lost. I was told in reply that the lashing was probably the work of some one who understood his business, superintended by an engineer officer or other expert in such matters. A day or two before we landed in Cuba my curiosity was aroused by a thronging of officers and men to one side of our vessel. Looking out on the water, I saw this lighter, loose and free, about half a mile from us, drifting ever farther away, and a small boat with a couple of men in it pulling out from our vessel towards it. There was hardly a breeze or a swell, and there had not been a storm during the voyage. But I was not surprised to learn afterwards that the other lighter was lost. This one would have been, too, had it got loose at night instead of in broad daylight. I wondered, as I saw it caught up and secured again, whether the same expert, who was charged with transferring the lighters to Cuba, was to direct the use of them there in unloading the vessels and constructing a landing.

71

On the day of our final start for Cuba, June 14th, I wrote home: "I understand that the Twentieth Infantry, probably the best regiment in the service, has been selected to take the advance in landing. I have no idea how much resistance will be met with, but I hope it will not be such as to require the energetic and skilful handling of our whole force. Of the twenty-five regiments of infantry and cavalry, I doubt whether two of the same brigade have ever practised attacking together, and whether half of them have ever practised attacking at all as regiments. The old blunders of the [Civil] War will be done over again with the same results. Lines of battle will be thrown against intrenched positions before the latter are accurately located; thin lines of skirmishers will find themselves suddenly overpowered with fire, and be repulsed before they can be supported; attacks will be commenced before arrangements are perfected for following up such advantage as may be gained. No general, concerted attack will be possible with our troops. To think otherwise is a gross slander on the art of war."

On the 17th, about three o'clock in the morning, I was waked up by the Major of my squadron, and notified that reveille would be sounded at daylight, if not before, and that my troop and the other troop of the squadron were to be formed with cartridge-belts and carbines along the starboard rail, and that two troops of the First Cavalry were to be formed on the other rail—ready to fire at torpedo-boats. I had noticed before this that the ship was rolling uncommonly. I soon found that the ship had stopped and become separated from the fleet. It turned out that a signal to halt had been made by one of the gunboats, or a signal made by one was interpreted as the signal to halt. At that time the Captain of the ship and his first officer had gone to bed, and the deck was under the charge of the mate. It was thought by some that he misunderstood the signal. At any rate, for three or four hours he circled around or stood stock-still looking for the fleet which he had allowed to pass out of his sight. The General did not know anything about it until the officer of the guard, a cavalry officer, woke him up and told him. I went on deck with my troop and remained with it at the rail until six, when I was relieved by another troop. Until four o'clock in the afternoon the deck was continually lined with men armed with carbines, the remainder of the command being confined between decks. I heard remarks made by officers to the effect that a commander who should cause a loaded transport to offer resistance to a torpedo-boat, or any other armed vessel, ought to be court-martialled. At three o'clock a vessel was sighted which proved to be the *City of Washington*, of our fleet, towing the water-boat. The remainder of the fleet came into view in the course of the afternoon.

Gambling being prohibited, and no games provided, or regular exercise required, the men found time hanging heavily on their hands. The chief events of the day were breakfast, dinner, and supper. For each meal the men formed in single file with their meat-ration cans, and got their wad of canned beef and handful of hard-tack. For dinner they had also canned beans or canned tomatoes as they came out of the can, uncooked and unwarmed, except by the air of the ship. At breakfast and supper they had coffee. Next to the coffee, what they liked best was the tomatoes. They grew very tired of the stringy, tasteless canned beef. Now and then an individual or organization would secure the use of the galley, and get a mess of something hot. It was suggested to me by one of my superior officers that I might give my troop a hot meal if I chose to " hustle " for it. I replied that if I were ordered to have a meal cooked, and told when I might have the galley, I would do so, but that I did not propose to do any " hustling." It moved me not only with pity, but with mortification, to see my men at the door of the officers' galley, begging or bargaining, as it seemed, for the remains of the officers' table. Between meals the principal occupations for the men were sleeping, or trying to sleep, and watching the other transports and the war-vessels. The bands did not devote much time to practising, and were handicapped for a time by the disability of several members from sea-sickness. But they played regularly, one in the morning and one in the evening. Men gathered about the band and applauded an occasional fine effort, or popular or patriotic air. "There'll be a hot time in the old town to-night" invariably evoked cheers and yells. Last piece of all came "The Star Spangled Banner," everybody standing, facing the stern, where the flag was slowly lowered. This imposing ceremony was followed by a bathos-like performance on a "tocsin of the soul." A lanky waiter in white apron popped out from under the bridge and tripped down to the main cabin tapping a gong to call the officers to dinner. The men who lined the edge of the hurricane-deck followed this individual with their eyes, and, having nothing else to applaud, applauded him. They did not mean to annoy their officers, but I, for one, felt a little uncomfortable as I thought of their cold stomachs, and the hot soup and meat and vegetables that I was going to put into mine.

On the morning of the 18th, we were delayed several hours waiting for the vessels to get together, as they had become widely scattered during the night. About 1 P.M. we came in sight of the coast of Cuba, and after that coursed along due westward parallel to it, and about ten miles from it. As we rounded Cape Maysi, the eastern end of Cuba (June 19th), we kept for some time a due south course, which made some of us think that our destination was not Santiago but Puerto Rico. On the 20th we brought up some five or ten miles off the southern coast of Cuba, and waited most of the day for something, we did not know what. We expected every moment to get orders to land. That evening two of the war-vessels went close to the shore and fired three or four shots. Soon afterwards a despatch-boat came close alongside of us, and some one on it called out: "Take cruising order: course southwest," and off we went southwestward. This was about 5.50 P.M. I did not know what our long inaction meant, unless it was that General Shafter had been trying to bring the Spanish commander to terms without a fight. No one seemed to know where we were going, but it was generally supposed that we were only placing ourselves out of reach of Spanish torpedo-boats. We stopped about eight o'clock.

On the morning of the 21st I found that we had not moved during the night. It had rained, and the sky was overcast. We could just make out the hazy forms of the mountains bordering the southern coast of Cuba. It was frightfully close and hot between decks aft, where my men and others slept (except those who slept on deck), and where they stood inspection twice a day, and got their meals. There was not a port, or bull's-eye, or anything of the kind open. No air reached that place except what came down the hatchway. The people of the ship pretended that it was dangerous to open the ports, but the General made them open one.

From what I saw, and statements made by the first officer of the ship, I judge that the crew did not number one-third of the hands that it should have numbered. There was no army officer on board, so far as I could learn, who knew the terms of the contract made by the steamship company with the government. So, when we were told that there was no change of sheets or towels for the state-rooms, and that the ice and other supplies had given out or run short, we did not know whether we had any right to complain or not. The steward told me that the Quarter-master or other officer who attended to fitting out the *Leona* told him that if he stocked his larder for a week, the supplies for the officers would be ample. We were a week on the vessel before we fairly started, and he never received any instructions to add to his stock. As we were on the vessel altogether two weeks, it is rather surprising that we fared as well as we did. Our travel-rations, which were issued only to include the 19th, were made to last to include breakfast on the 21st. There were plenty of rations in the hold, but no more travel-rations. What additional rations we issued would have to be cooked.

VIII

DAIQUIRI

ABOUT 1 P.M. on the 21st the troop commanders were informed that the troops would land at daylight on the 22d. At a quarter of six, about an hour after daylight, on the 22d, the *Leona* was about five miles from land. The original instructions were for the men to take with them in landing two days' rations and one hundred cartridges per man, each troop to leave two men behind to look after the troop property on board. About seven o'clock we were ordered to take *all* our ammunition and leave *three* men behind. About eight o'clock we were again ordered to take only one hundred cartridges per man. It was ordered that each troop should take three axes, three picks, and three shovels, to be carried by the men. These articles and the rations had to be gotten out of the hold. If we had been told when we went aboard what we would be required to have when we went ashore, we might have kept these things out of the hold, or disposed them so that they could be easily gotten at. Having already told how the things were put into the hold, it is hardly necessary to describe the efforts by which we got out our bacon, coffee, and hard bread, and picks, axes, and shovels. It was like a swarm of ants whose hill has been stirred up with a stick, except that in the case of the ants one cannot hear or understand what they are saying nor see or imagine the sweat and grime.

The *Leona* moved in towards the shore, and the General was notified which vessel we should follow in landing. The following is a copy of the order for disembarkation:

General Orders, }   HEADQUARTERS FIFTH ARMY CORPS,
No. 18.   }   ON BOARD S. S." SEGURANCA," AT SEA,
June 20, 1898.

1. Under instructions to be communicated to the proper commanders, troops will disembark in the following order:

First. The Second Division, Fifth Corps (Lawton's). The Gatling-gun detachment will accompany this division.

Second. General Bates's brigade. This brigade will form as a reserve to the Second Division, Fifth Corps.

Third. The dismounted cavalry division (Wheeler's).

Fourth. The First Division, Fifth Corps (Kent's).

Fifth. The [mounted] squadron of the Second Cavalry (Rafferty's).

Sixth. If the enemy in force vigorously resist the landing, the light artillery, or part of it, will be disembarked by the battalion commander and brought to the assistance of the troops engaged. If no serious opposition be offered, this artillery will be unloaded after the mounted squadron (Rafferty's).

2. All troops will carry on the person the blanket-roll (with shelter-tent and poncho), three days' field-rations (with coffee, ground), canteens filled, and one hundred rounds of ammunition per man. Additional ammunition, already issued to the troops, tentage, baggage, and company cooking utensils, will be left under charge of the regimental Quartermaster, with one non-commissioned officer and two privates from each company.

3. All persons not immediately on duty with, and constituting a part of, the organizations mentioned in the foregoing paragraphs, will remain aboard ship until the landing be accomplished, and until notified they can land.

4. The chief Quartermaster of the expedition will control all small boats, and will distribute them to the best advantage to disembark the troops in the order indicated in paragraph 1.

5. The ordnance officer, Second Lieutenant Brooke, Fourth Infantry, will put on shore, at once, one hundred rounds of ammunition per man, and have it ready for distribution on the firing-line.

6. The commanding General wishes to impress officers and men with the crushing effect a well-directed fire will have upon the Spanish troops. All officers concerned will rigidly enforce fire discipline, and will caution their men to fire only when they can see the enemy.

*　　*　　*　　*　　*　　*　　*

By command of Major-General Shafter :

E. J. McCLERNAND,
Assistant Adjutant-General.

By night about six thousand troops were on shore. General Lawton was ordered to push down a strong force to seize and hold Siboney. [Report of Major-General Shafter.]

DAIQUIRI

We halted among the other transports. The water between and beyond the transports was dotted with small boats loaded with troops, with their packs on and their carbines or rifles standing upright in front of them. Here and there were strings of small boats fastened to steam - launches with machine - guns in the bows. The swell of the sea, which scarcely moved the heavy transports, made these little craft dance. There seemed to be no order, or formation, either of the transports or of the small boats. They lay or moved about as if waiting for somebody to straighten them out and tell them what to do. Suddenly, bang, bang, bang went the guns of two or three war-vessels. With intense interest and delight the troops caught the flash and smoke of shot after shot, and the dust thrown up on the shore, now close to the water's edge in and about the little town of Daiquiri, now on the wooded sides of the hills behind it, now on a rocky point to the right of the town, as we looked at it, whence a block-house frowned down on the town and adjacent water. After this cannonade had lasted about thirty minutes without being replied to, it ceased, and a few small boats moved in to the shore, and deposited the first party of troops. While others were closely following these, all eyes were of a sudden attracted to the rocky point overlooking Daiquiri, where the stars and stripes were being flung to the breeze. Immediately the air was filled with cheers, and whoops, and yells, the shrieking of whistles and crashing of brass bands. The landing of men went on the rest of the day. The mules for the wagons and pack-trains were mostly thrown overboard and left to swim ashore, and few, I understand, were lost.

This afternoon (June 22d) our regiment went from the *Leona* onto a large tug, which took us to the unfinished dock at which we landed. Many of the men had to jump from the vessel to the dock, and afterwards from plank to plank. Two men of our regiment had already been drowned here, and it is a wonder that no more were lost. The regiment remained standing in the road about half an hour, during which time, as I understood, the Adjutant hunted around for a place for it to camp in, there being no one present to direct him to one. It was almost dark when we reached it and disposed ourselves in a way to fit into it.

I was looking at this time for a general order congratulating the troops on the success of the expedition thus far, commending them for their behavior on the transports, giving them some information about the enemy, and perhaps a hint at the plan of operation, and appealing to their pride and ambition to answer the extraordinary demands about to be made upon them. As many of the officers and men had never been in the presence of their commanding General, I thought there would be a review, or that the General would take occasion to ride with his staff along the front of the troops drawn up in line, so that he could see them, and they him. But there was no inspiring or congratulatory order; and I, for one, never saw General Shafter during the campaign.

We had, as directed, three days' rations in our haversacks. The men were in blue flannel shirts and blue cloth trousers and leggings, having left their blouses on board. Each man carried half a shelter-tent, one blanket, and a poncho or slicker. A poncho is a rubber blanket with a slit in the middle to put the head through so that it can be worn like a cape.

The officers had, like the men, to carry their own baggage, except that the field and staff officers, being mounted, threw the burden of it on their horses. I understood that at the end of three days, or about that time, we would have the tentage that we had left in the hold of the transport, and so I did not provide myself with a shelter-tent or blanket. All the covering I had with me was a light rubber overcoat. I had a haversack* containing three days' rations, a

* To be strictly correct, I had a clothing-bag which I used as a haversack. Clothing-bags were issued in lieu of haversacks to our regiment, and, I believe, to the

meat-ration can, and knife, fork, and spoon, also a canteen and a tin cup.

Early the next morning (June 23d) our First Squadron went on towards Santiago to connect with the advance. My troop remained with the Second Squadron at Daiquiri. Bands of Cubans in ragged and dirty white linen, barefooted, and variously armed, marched past us, carrying Cuban and American flags. Our officers and men lined the road to see them and cheer them. The Cubans were evidently undisciplined. I thought from their appearance that they would probably prove useful as guides and scouts, but that we would have to do practically all the fighting. It was understood that about one thousand of them were to meet us at Daiquiri. About seventy-five, I was told, were all that turned up.*

No sinks were constructed in our camp. Our drinking and cooking water was taken from a

other regiments. There is no material difference between the two.

* On the 23d the disembarkation was continued, and about six thousand more men landed. Early on this date General Lawton's advance reached Siboney, the Spanish garrison of about six hundred men retiring as he came up, and offering no opposition except a few scattering shots at long range. Some of the Cuban troops pursued the retreating Spaniards and skirmished with them.

creek. I went down to it, and found men bathing and washing their clothes at intervals along the bank, and others filling their canteens not far from them. There was no guard or patrol to prevent the pollution of the water. The evening of the 23d we replenished our haversacks so as to be supplied for three days. The ration consisted, as long as I was in Cuba, of coffee, hard bread, canned beef or bacon, and sugar. The coffee was issued unground. When a man got his little pile he would take it off and pound it between two stones. It is hardly necessary to say that the grounds were coarse, entailing considerable loss in cooking. Orders were issued for us to boil all our drinking-water. We had nothing to boil anything in but our tin cups, which held about one-third of the contents of a canteen. There was not time to boil the water between breakfast and starting on the march, unless we started pretty late; and when we did boil our water, we had warm water to drink the rest of the day. I tried at first to boil mine, and to have my men boil theirs, but I soon gave it up as impracticable.

There were three kinds of fruit which grew in considerable quantity in this country—the mango, the cocoanut, and the lime. It was generally understood that the mango was for us an unwholesome fruit. The Cubans seemed to live on it, and many of our men could not be restrained from eating it. Although cautioned by their officers against it, they would bring it into camp by the hatful. Many got cramps and diarrhœa from it. The cocoanut was also generally regarded as injurious, but eaten by many nevertheless. I was told, however, by an expert, that the milk of the *green* cocoanut was perfectly wholesome. All our advisers agreed in recommending the lime, ripe or green, and in any quantity. The juice of this fruit was the most palatable thing that passed my lips in Cuba.

This evening (June 23d) we had our first taste of tropical rain. Kennington and I had retired for the night to an arbor which we had constructed to protect us against the sun. It had not rained long when drip, drip, the first drops came through our saturated roof. We got up, gathered our overcoats about us, and took seats on a cracker-box or our saddles—I do not remember which. The drippings from our hats and shoulders accumulated in pools in our laps and around our points of support. It has been truly said that nothing takes the spirit out of a soldier like wetting the seat of his breeches. When our wetting had quite reached this demoralizing stage, the rain stopped, and the stars came out, twinkling, it seemed, with enjoyment. We were glad to take a place at the fire which the men started up, and dry our clothes with them, and listen to their chaff, until we got to the part of our clothing which we habitually sit upon. At that point we had a fire made for the officers, and modestly retired to complete our drying and dressing.

IX

ON the morning of the 24th we took up our march towards Santiago. Officers and men were more or less debilitated by the long confinement aboard ship. They were unaccustomed to foot-marching, especially with packs on their backs. It was therefore surprising that we did not start until after eight o'clock. Our route was a rough, narrow road with many a steep ascent. We marched through the hottest part of the day. The dense undergrowth kept us, when we halted, from getting the shelter of the woods on either side of us. We would occasionally pass a regiment of infantry resting by the side of the road, and pay them back as well as we could for the chaffing they would subject us to on account of our being afoot. Knapsacks, blankets, and shelter-tents were strewn along the road. Here and there we would pass a man lying down overcome by the heat, or pretending to be. In the latter part of our march we passed bands of Cuban insurgents resting or in bivouac, and a number of Cuban individuals driving donkeys loaded with

LAS GUASIMAS

cast-off U. S. blankets.   I heard afterwards that,
back near our starting-point, a party of our men
lay in ambush for these fellows, and made them
give up their plunder.

About the middle of the afternoon a stream of
litter-bearers passed us, taking wounded to the
rear.   Shortly afterwards we crossed a creek and
came upon the field of Las Guasimas.*   The

* This engagement was brought on, against the wishes
and intentions of General Shafter, by General Wheeler,
commanding the cavalry division, of which at this time
little more than one brigade (Young's) was landed. "The
orders for June 24th contemplated General Lawton's
division taking a strong defensive position a short distance from Siboney, on the road to Santiago; Kent's
division was to be held near Siboney, where he disembarked; Bates's brigade was to take position in support
of Lawton, while Wheeler's division was to be somewhat
to the rear on the road from Siboney to Daiquiri. It was
intended to maintain this situation until the troops and
transportation were disembarked and a reasonable quantity of necessary supplies landed." [Report of Major-
General Shafter.]   I cannot doubt that General Shafter
intended to proceed along the coast to the entrance of
Santiago harbor, and open it for our fleet, but changed
his line of march in consequence of General Wheeler's
eccentric movement.   It has been asserted that General
Wheeler was in command of all the troops on shore, but
he was not.   He commanded only the troops of his own
division, and it was with these troops that he marched
past Lawton and ordered the enemy to be attacked
at Las Guasimas. [Report of Major-General Wheeler,
June 26, 1898.]

ground was admirably adapted to the purpose for which the enemy had chosen it. On our right was the steep side of a mountain, on the top of which two or three block-houses could be made out at intervals of about half a mile. On our left a succession of rugged hills extended to the sea. The country was generally covered with dense wood and undergrowth. Immediately adjoining the creek were a few acres of comparatively level, open ground. A single ruin of a house stood on the right of the road about fifty yards from the creek, and a house on the same side of the road, about fifty yards beyond the ruin. Officers of the Tenth, who were in the engagement, gave me their accounts of it, and from what they said, and what I have read about it, I have formed a general idea of how it went. Our plan of attack, I understand, was determined the evening before at brigade headquarters, the presence and position of the enemy having been reported there. From Siboney the troops advanced in two columns, the right column, consisting of a squadron of the First and one of the Tenth Cavalry took the road which we had taken and which led against the enemy's front; the left column, consisting of the Rough Riders, took a road leading against the enemy's right. In the right column the First Cavalry had the advance. When it was about a mile and a half from the creek the men were warned that they were approaching the enemy, and cautioned to make as little noise as possible. As they crossed the creek, they came under vigorous volley-firing, which was kept up throughout the action. Our men deployed under a galling fire, and rapidly advanced, firing at will. The enemy was formed in two lines. His first line occupied the crest of a hill about two hundred feet high and about one thousand yards from the creek. This line commanded the road by which our right column had marched. His second line was about eight hundred yards in rear of the first. It commanded both of the roads used by our troops. The two lines numbered about twenty-four hundred men. Our squadrons were broken up, so that the command of the organizations was practically left to the eight troop commanders, four of the First Cavalry and four of the Tenth. About half an hour after the ball opened, the fire of the Rough Riders was heard on the left. They came into action against the enemy's right, about six hundred yards to the left and rear of a troop of the Tenth Cavalry, which was on the left of the First Cavalry. The other troops of the Tenth Cavalry were on the right of the First. The enemy retreated in time to prevent our taking any prisoners, but leaving a number of their dead where they fell. I heard that the Rough Riders were in position to have cut off a hundred or more of the enemy, but let them pass on their calling out "Cubanos," also that a supporting line of the Rough Riders fired into the firing line, killing an officer and a number of men. These statements, I believe, have been contradicted. I heard, too, that while our men were fighting, our Cuban allies robbed them of everything that they had in their haversacks, which they took off and left behind when they went into action.

All the artillery that we had on the field consisted of four Hotchkiss guns, manned by men of the Tenth Cavalry and commanded by Captain Watson of the Tenth Cavalry. Only three pieces were in action. They fired upon the enemy's first line from a position on the low, open ground near the ruin.

We remained encamped on the field of Las Guasimas from June 24th to June 26th. Orders were issued prohibiting bathing in the stream from which we got our drinking-water. I understand that there was water near by in which we were allowed to bathe, but I did not learn of it while I was there, and I do not believe that many of the officers or men did.

The afternoon of the 25th, Watson and I, feeling our mouths watering for limes, scrambled through some stiff underbrush, climbed a tree, and filled our pockets with them. I had a number of them in the bottom of my haversack for several days afterwards.

No sinks were constructed in this camp until the evening of the 25th. As we left the next morning, they were not of much use.

X

SEVILLA

FROM Las Guasimas we marched over the high ground from which the Spaniards had been driven. Before commencing our descent, some of us, stepping a little to one side of the column, caught a glimpse of the town of Santiago, a scattering of light-colored houses encircled with green hills backed by mountains of a darker shade. A ridge on our left cut off the harbor and the sea from our view. We halted at a place called Sevilla, marked by a single ruined house and a couple of gate-posts. Again we stood about half an hour waiting for instructions. There seemed to be no one ahead to ascertain or determine where we should halt and camp. Throughout the campaign the marching was unnecessarily fatiguing from its not being properly regulated. When the column came to a halt there was no telling whether it was to rest or to wait for the way to be cleared. The troops did not know whether they should lay off their packs or not. Sometimes, after standing with them on for several minutes, they would take them off, and about the time they had done so the march would be resumed. So far as I know, there was no order issued regarding the rate of marching, frequency or duration of the halts, or intervals between organizations, etc., and, as a general thing, no signal or other means was employed to communicate with the rear when the head of the column halted to rest or when it resumed the march.

In our new camp we were about eight miles from Santiago and about six miles from its intrenchments. We could not see the place from the camp, but I got a view of it from a spur of the mountain on our right, and from a point of a ridge about a mile to our front on the left, where we had pickets. We were camped on the right of the road. Other regiments, infantry and cavalry, camped on both sides of the road in rear and in advance of us. Four batteries of field-artillery came up, and went into camp near us on the opposite side of the road. They were very much better off as to tentage, rations, and cooking-utensils than the infantry and cavalry. I understood at this time that we would have to wait for our siege artillery to come up before we could attack Santiago. I heard officers say that siege-guns could not be brought up by the road that we had travelled, and others say that they would engage to bring them up by it if they were allowed to do so. I heard also that the siege-guns could not be gotten off the transports for want of lighters, and that they would be of no use if they were gotten off and brought up, because the breech-blocks, hindsights, or some other necessary parts, had been left in the United States.

We had no outposts on our flanks, and what we had in our front were, from all that I could see or learn, a mere point, or advance-guard. But "all's well that ends well." The Spaniards might have annoyed our camps a good deal, but did not trouble us at all. There was some patrolling beyond our outposts, but no reconnaissance in force. I was ordered once to take my troop out for patrol duty to the point where the creek which we were camped on crossed the road, and wait there for the arrival of the brigade commander. This, I thought, was to be my first practical experience in patrolling. I had been in the army twenty-five years, but had never commanded a patrol in the presence of an enemy— real, represented, or imagined. I told off the men who were to form the advance party, flanking parties, and rear-guard, and started off in column, intending to take the formation prescribed in books for a patrol when I should approach the outposts. Having passed one or two camps and proceeded some distance without seeing any troops to my right or left, Kennington inquired of me whether we had passed the outposts. I replied that I did not suppose I had, but did not know. He then suggested that I form as patrol, and I did so. On arriving at the creek, I found a sentinel or two posted on the near bank. I forded it and halted on the opposite bank to await the arrival of the brigade commander. I concealed my men in the dense underbrush on the sides of the road, in ambush against any hostile party that might come along, and cautioned them to take prisoners rather than to kill. When the brigade commander arrived he told me that the patrol would not be needed, as a party of Cubans had gone on down the road and would answer the purpose of the patrol. As I crossed the creek, going back, I heard an officer, who had evidently taken charge of the guard at the ford, say that the sentinels did not know where the adjoining post was on their right or left, nor the ground in their front, nor what they were to do— in fact, did not know anything about their duties except that they were to remain where they were. Here and at other points where I came upon our pickets, I could not see anything that looked like supports. On my return to camp First Sergeant Givens came up to me with a private of the troop, saluted, and reported that this man, being a member of a flanking party, had sat down and remained behind while the troop went on towards the creek. I shall never forget the expression of mingled contempt and indignation, tempered with respect for me, with which he

said, " Such a man isn't fit to be a soldier." It
was one of our recruits. I detailed him for all
the fatigue duty that should come up in the troop
for six weeks.

During our stay here, which lasted from the
26th until the 30th of June, we had rain about
every day, and heavy dew every night. My feet
were almost continually wet. On the 29th, Captain Grierson of the Tenth gave me a shelter-
tent and a blanket which he had to spare. Until
then I had no protection, night or day, under me
or over me, but my rubber overcoat, and the
branches of trees. When it rained I got out in
the open, stooped down so that the bottom
of my overcoat would reach the ground, and
"took it." Kennington and I luxuriated in the
tent.

The men were not allowed to bathe in the
creek, which was the only water available. I got
the only bath that I had in Cuba by digging a
trough by the side of the creek, laying my rubber
overcoat in it, and filling it from the creek with
my tin cup.

The road was almost continually alive with
troops, wagons, mule-trains, couriers, and staff-
officers, going or coming. I would often stroll
down to it, and stand among a lot of soldiers looking on at the shifting mass of men, animals, and
vehicles, occasionally recognizing an organization
or an individual, and greeting an acquaintance or

being greeted by one whom I had not recognized. It was thus that I met my good friend Hersey, of the Twelfth Foot, who gave me something for my mess from the wagon-load of commissaries which he was hustling up from Siboney; and the noble, lovable young Michie, whom I had known from his childhood, and was never to see again, for he was to fall among the first on the deadly slope of San Juan Hill. I remember seeing the Second Massachusetts go by, and being impressed by the improvement of the men in appearance since I saw them at Lakeland. They were about as brown, and looked almost as hardy, as the Regulars. They went through mud and water, well closed up, at a good swinging gait. Our Volunteers in Cuba, as a class, did themselves credit. They had not the respect for shoulder-straps that is desirable—nor had the Regulars—but they were much better soldiers than Volunteers of our Civil War with the same length of service. I am bound to say that they did better on the march and in action than I had expected them to.

On the 27th I was informed by the regimental Adjutant that officers were no longer required to carry their sabres. I had carried mine, against my wishes, one thousand miles. There was no way for me to rid myself of it now except to throw it in the bushes, and pay for it when the campaign should be over; for it was a government sabre, belonging to the troop. I determined to keep on carrying it.

During the night of the 27th I was awakened by the squadron commander and told to have my men dress, but remain in their tents, and hold themselves in readiness to turn out under arms. After I had done so, and had stood armed, with my Lieutenant, for some time, waiting for something interesting and exciting, I was told to let all hands go to sleep again. It was reported the next morning that the guard of the Seventy-first New York, camped near us, had caused this interruption of our slumbers by firing into one of its own patrols. Such an occurrence is naturally incidental to campaigning with troops who learn the art of war in the presence of the enemy.

Rations were issued very irregularly. We might on the same day receive two days' coffee, one day's bread, and three days' bacon. Sometimes we received only the fraction of a day's allowance of one or more of the components of our short ration, such as half a day's sugar. It got so that the company commanders could no longer keep account of their rations, and differed or disagreed among themselves as to what they had. Rations were issued pro rata as they came up from the rear. There were no scales to measure anything with, and the brigade commissary had to get experienced non-commissioned officers to judge for him the weight of sides of bacon, sacks of flour, etc. The men did not on an average get the full allowance even of coffee, bread, bacon, or canned beef, and what they got did not go as far as it ordinarily would, because of the wastage due to individual cooking. It was impossible to cook for the troop collectively, as we had no kettles or other cooking-utensils, except the tin cups and mess-pans carried by the men individually. I have vague, indistinct recollections of complaints about the beef, but did not take the trouble to investigate them. I disliked the beef myself, and I had no reason to suppose that the men liked it any better than I did, and I was morally certain that no good would come from my complaining about it. I once had an experience as a complainant to the War Department, which I did not care to have repeated. It was about the year 1893. I was in command of Troop F, of the Tenth Cavalry. An appurtenance of the carbine (front sight cover) having proved itself to me too fragile for use in active service, I reported the fact to the Chief of Ordnance, and requested that a more durable one, which had been, and I thought was still, issued by the Ordnance Department, be furnished me for my troop. I was informed in reply that I was the first officer to make any complaint about the front sight cover, and that was all the satisfaction I got. In case I had complained about the beef, I should probably have been the first officer to do so. These particulars of my humble experience may suggest a possible explanation of General Miles's inaction for a time in the matter of beef. Staff-officers, having horses or mules to ride, would make trips back to Siboney, and come up with their saddle-pockets crammed with good things, such as canned beans, tomatoes, and salt. We felt the want of salt very much. At last a limited supply of commissary stores came up for sale to officers. I laid in a stock of canned beans and tomatoes, rice, dried beans, bacon, sugar, salt, etc., which I could not have gotten into three haversacks, and we got orders to march that afternoon. I ate boiled rice and canned tomatoes until I was ready to burst, and, after I had packed my haversack full, gave what supplies I had left to my First Sergeant.

General Shafter, who came up to the front the day before, assembled the division commanders at his headquarters this afternoon, and communicated to them his plan of battle. General Wheeler, being ill with fever, was not present. The cavalry division was represented by General Sumner, the next in rank. It is a curious fact that while General Wheeler was thus excluded from the conference, General Shafter was hardly in better physical condition than General Wheeler. He was about as badly disabled by the heat as General Hooker was by the blow he received from a pillar of the Chancellorsville House on the 3d of May, 1863, but, like Hooker, he continued, notwithstanding his disability, to direct or determine the operations of the army. This circumstance accounts, in a measure, for the remarkable fact that no order, circular, letter, or memorandum, not a scrap of paper, has yet come to light which shows, in writing, what the plan of battle was *before the event*.

XI

EL POZO

I HAD heard that there were stacks of mail at Şiboney waiting to be sorted and sent to the front, and on the 29th expected that I would receive my first mail in Cuba on the 30th. I was particularly interested in a registered letter from my wife, containing money. But on the 30th we took up our march again, and my mail never overtook me in Cuba. When my troop formed for the march from Sevilla, some of the men failed to put their full packs on, intending to leave certain articles, such as blankets, shelter-tents, etc., behind. I told them that they ought not to start without them, that we would probably not make a long march, and it would be time enough to throw such things away when they found that they could not carry them any farther. They then picked up the articles referred to and secured them to their packs. I do not believe that they afterwards threw them away. My pack was larger and heavier than ever, but I prized its contents and toted it cheerfully. We marched as usual, alternately in

single and double file, by the same single road,
lined with dense wood and undergrowth. About
the middle of the march we had to halt about
half an hour while an infantry regiment filed
across the road, cutting our column in two. In
the mean time we sat around their abandoned
camp-fires, smoking and chatting, and watching
the passing columns and the war balloon, which
we saw go up for the first time. Resuming the
march, we soon commenced going up a hill to
our left. We passed a building which I afterwards learned was known as El Pozo, and near
which a battery of artillery (Grimes's) had gone
into camp. Having wound our way a few hundred
yards farther up the hill we halted near the
summit. In our front, after forming line to the
right, the ground sloped rapidly away into the
basin in which lay Santiago and El Caney. But I
did not realize at the time that we were within two
or three miles of these places or their defences.
It was after dark when we went into camp. We
were not allowed to light fires. Most of the men
turned in without eating. Kennington and I
got out our canned commissaries, and made a
good supper, for a cold one.

For the first time in the campaign our regiment
put out pickets. Lieutenant Smith had his
troop out immediately in front of mine, which
was, if necessary, to support his. In the morning I relieved his troop with mine. He took me

through the dense shrubbery by a labyrinth, which I could hardly have found out alone, to each of his posts. I can see his broad shoulders and frank, manly face now as he halts in sight of one of his sentinels, and with a look directs my attention to him. When my last sentinel was posted he left me, and I never saw him again, and never can in this world; for a few hours later a Spanish bullet ended his noble life, as he arrived with his men on the crest of San Juan Hill. Observing a ridge about one hundred yards from our position, and about parallel to it, and thinking that we might have to advance over it, I thought I would explore the intervening ground, and take a look at the ridge itself and the ground beyond it. I had hardly started towards it with a patrol, headed by Sergeant Elliot, when I received an order to withdraw my troop and fall in with the squadron in marching order.

About the time I got my troop in its place in the column we heard firing of infantry, and caught sight of our lines closing in on El Caney. Now and then a boom and a puff of smoke told of a shot from our artillery. The officers and men watched these operations standing with their packs on in the road waiting for the order to march. Some of them could make out what our artillery was firing at, and occasionally see where a shot struck, but I could not. Pretty soon the enemy commenced firing with artillery, and the

report of his bursting shell sounded very distinctly to us. I heard afterwards that some of
them struck the building of El Pozo, on the roof
of which a party of Cubans were watching the
contest, and the result was a great scattering of
Cubans. Some casualties too were caused in the
artillery posted here. About this time a group of
foreign attachés, driven away by the same fire
from the position of El Pozo, came up to where
we stood, and took position near a large tree in
our front. I remember particularly the fine, stal-
wart figure of Captain William Paget, the British
Naval Attaché, and his spy-glass. Shortly before
we started to descend into the basin, I heard him
say to his companions that he thought the position that they then had was about the best that
they could take up to watch the operations from.

After waiting about an hour for orders, our
regiment took up the march. I thought as I
passed El Pozo that the place looked a little different from what it did the evening before, but I
had no idea that it had been the target of the
enemy's artillery. We wound our way down
into the basin, and pushed on at a brisk pace in
the direction of San Juan. I did not know where
we were going nor what we were to do. I understand that our Colonel did not know either.
In the basin we found other troops moving in the
same direction as we were and by the same road.
When we halted for rest, other troops would pass

us, and when they halted we would pass them. I remember seeing a Gatling battery, and, I believe, a battery of artillery, pass us. At times our regiment and another regiment, each in column of files or twos, would be marching abreast in the narrow road. At one time our regiment, a regiment of infantry, and a train of pack-mules were all abreast, going in the same direction. They must have been in single file. There seemed to be less management or more mismanagement of the marching columns to-day than on any previous day. I was joined on the march by the distinguished narrator of the operations which I was helping to execute, Mr. Richard Harding Davis, who accompanied me some distance. We remarked, as we passed the cluster of large tents of the Division Hospital, that it smelt like an apothecary shop. I little thought then that I would be lying in one of them that night. I remember my old friend Major Mc-Clernand, General Shafter's Adjutant-General, passing me on his way from the direction of El Caney, and calling out, " Hullo, Bigelow! they are doing well out there, but they need you." I hardly expected even then to take an active part in the fighting.

XII

UNDER FIRE

SUDDENLY the column halted, and we were told to strip ourselves of everything but arms and ammunition, which we proceeded to do. I have seen it stated, in explanation of the suffering from hunger in front of Santiago, that the men threw away their haversacks when they went into action. I did not see any haversacks thrown away. The rolls, haversacks, and canteens of my men were taken off and laid on the ground by order of the squadron commander, who undoubtedly had the order from the regimental commander. I left two men of my troop with the packs to prevent their being plundered by our Cuban allies. I took this occasion to relieve myself of my sabre, running it about six inches deep into the soft ground, by the side of my pack, and leaving it sticking there. I have never seen it since, nor my pack either.

About this time our balloon, which had been up about half an hour, commenced coming down near the right of our regiment. A figure could be seen in the basket, leaning over the side, evidently communicating with some one on terra firma. When it got about one hundred feet from the ground, a loud crashing and sputtering sound was heard, and the speed of its descent was noticeably accelerated. It came to the ground, and I did not see it go up again. I have heard that it was riddled with shrapnel bullets. At the same time that this occurred a whirring sound struck our ears, which we needed no experience to know was that of volleys of small-calibre rifles directed down the road. As the bullets tore through the dense foliage about us, we caught sight here and there of a piece of leaf floating gracefully down to the ground, indicating about where the centre of impact had passed. At the first volley, being entirely unprepared for it, I ducked my head involuntarily, and felt as if I must, or ought to, be hit. On realizing that I was not, I was pleased to observe that no one seemed to have noticed me. I am pretty sure that nobody did. Every one was doubtless absorbed just then in his own sensations and deportment. After that I did not attempt to dodge bullets, though I repeatedly sought shelter from them. About as we received the first volley of infantry fire the troop ahead of mine started to the rear, but was soon checked. I understand that the impulse to retreat was imparted to it by the Seventy-first New York.

As one of the regiments with its packs on—I imagine it was the Sixth Infantry—swung heav-

ily by us at double-time, I heard above its rhyth-
mic *thud*, thud, *thud*, thud, one of the men call
out, " Stand aside, and let the infantry go to the
front," and I remember being nettled by the re-
mark.   I wondered why we were standing still
and this regiment going by us to the front.   Our
loads being disposed of, we were closed up, and
made to lie down in the road facing to the left.
Bullets kept tearing through the grass, bushes,
and branches about us.   They seemed mostly to
come from the direction of San Juan, enfilading
the road in which we lay.   I apprehended that
the enemy had taken this road as his target, and
had its direction about right, if he had not quite
gotten our range.   I looked around for a field-
officer to apply to for permission to take my men
to one side of the road, or at least face them in
the direction from which the fire was principally
coming.   My squadron commander had gone
towards our right, probably to confer with the
regimental commander, and there was no field-
officer in sight.   I therefore, on my own responsibility, changed front with my troop to the right.
In this position I was free from the troop lately
on my right, in case it should again break to the
rear.   I was under the impression that we were
much nearer the enemy than afterwards proved to
be the case, and expected the regiment to deploy
across the road at any minute.   From my studying of tactics and the drill regulations, together

with my limited experience in field-exercises, I knew that in dismounted fighting, especially in a densely wooded country, the time comes when the direction of operations is necessarily left to company commanders, and I judged that this time had come, or could not be far off. I did not know but that the squadron commander was disabled, and I was determined that my men should not be decimated without doing some execution, through fear of responsibility or lack of initiative on my part. I felt that I would be erring on the right side if I slightly anticipated the proper time for independent action by company commanders. After waiting a minute or two in my new position, the enemy's fire not abating, and no superior officer appearing, I faced my troop to the left, and pushed in single file into the wood far enough to clear the road by about ten or twenty yards with the rear of my column, when I came upon a line of infantry skirmishers, apparently a company without officers. The non-commissioned officers seemed at a loss which way to turn. I had my troop face to the right, or in the general direction in which the road ran, the direction of San Juan, and prepared to advance. During all this time I could not see San Juan or anything else farther than about twenty yards off. In anticipation of the difficulty of penetrating the dense undergrowth, I took immediate charge of the platoon commanded by my First Sergeant, William H. Givens, leaving the other one to Second Lieutenant J. F. Kennington, Tenth Cavalry, with instructions to keep this platoon in touch with mine. I then proceeded to advance in a direction parallel to the road which I had just left. I expected that by the time I arrived abreast of the head of my regiment I would find it deployed or deploying.

As we pushed on under the enemy's "unaimed" fire, now creeping and crawling through masses of vines and shrubbery, now wriggling through a wire fence, now rushing across open spots from one bush or copse to another, I called out to the men, "Move towards the sound of that firing!" pointing in the general direction of San Juan. "We'll soon get to open ground, where we'll see the enemy and have a chance to shoot back." The woods and thickets of Cuba have been described and spoken of as impenetrable. I have never seen the woods or thickets that I believed or found to be impenetrable for dismounted skirmishers. In my judgment, most of our manœuvring or marching on the field of San Juan might have been done off the roads or through the woods. The enemy, of course, had the roads under concentrated fire, especially where they forked or crossed the streams. Woods are generally a greater advantage to the offensive than they are to the defensive, because they favor secret or concealed manœuvring. But if the woods are so dense that they cannot be penetrated, or the offensive has not the enterprise and energy to manœuvre in them, they are an advantage to the defensive, as they confine the enemy to narrow defiles. Such was the case in the operations in which I was now participating. If the offensive does not manœuvre off the roads, and the defensive does, the latter seizes the initiative and secures the double advantage of having the enemy in long, thin columns, and of attacking him unawares. Such was the case at Chancellorsville; and if there had been a Stonewall Jackson and Robert E. Lee at Santiago, the same would have been the case there.

Bullets kept swishing past us, and now and then a shell burst overhead, but we could see nothing to fire at, and had been cautioned against firing, as troops of our own were in front of us. We waded a stream knee-deep, and, not far beyond it, came upon a road running towards San Juan, in which troops were lying facing in the direction of El Caney, but they were not the Tenth Cavalry. While we lay here resting Sergeant Dyals, of my troop, came to me from the right. He reported that Lieutenant Kennington was in that direction with his platoon, and asked, with the Lieutenant's compliments, whether he should join me. The bullets were coming pretty fast and thick down the road, and I did not wish to subject his platoon to any unnecessary loss, so I answered in the negative. Sergeant Dyals was afterwards wounded so that he lost the sight of one eye. He has since been discharged for physical disability.

Leaving this line behind us, we pushed on through a narrow belt of trees and bushes running along the road, and came out in an open field of rank grass nearly waist-high, and the sound of firing seemed to grow louder on our left. So I faced my men to the left, and filed off in that direction. As a number of bullets dropped near us, Sergeant Elliot, of my platoon, came up to me, and, pointing to a tree on our right, said, " Captain, I see something stirring in that tree ; it looks like a Spaniard. I'd like to shoot at it." I took a good look at the tree ; it was so dense I could not see into it. " It may be a Cuban," I said, " or one of our men. You had better not shoot," or something to that effect, and we went on. Soon afterwards, while we were lying down, Private Stovall was shot through the heart. He turned over and died, exclaiming, " God o' mercy ! God o' mercy ! God o' mercy !" The same bullet that killed him went through the hip and lodged in the thigh of Private Bledsoe. About two weeks afterwards Stovall's body, swollen from decomposition, and its eyes plucked out, was found hid in the tall grass where we left it.

Many a noble fellow dropped and died that day,
as Stovall did, perforce unnoticed by "the Captain" whom he was blindly and loyally following.
Who can estimate the responsibility of leading
men in battle? About one hundred yards farther
on we came upon a squad of infantrymen sitting
in the shade of trees around an officer who was
lying on his back bleeding from the face. While
we stood there conferring with these men, I
heard one of them say to another, "I guess he's
dead now." I believe that this officer and Private
Stovall were both shot by the sharp-shooter whom
Sergeant Elliot wanted to skirmish with. The
infantrymen told us that the Spaniards were advancing and our men falling back. We could
not see either. For a few moments I was afraid
that we were cut off, and destined to be carried
into Santiago as prisoners or massacred where we
were. On our left was a stream, probably the
one which we had already forded, and from the
other side of it came sounds of voices and loud
reports of firing. We could not tell whether
they were Spanish or American, but thought we
had better take our chances on their being
American. So we quickly waded the stream
and scrambled up the opposite bank, helping one
another, as it was about as high as a man and
quite steep. I believe I was the first one to
recognize through the thickets in our front the
uniform of our troops, which I did by the stripes

on the officers' and non-commissioned officers' trousers. Pushing on a short distance, we came upon a road lined with our infantry. It was on the far edge of the woods, and beyond it stretched a plain about six hundred yards wide, overgrown with tall grass like that through which we had lately passed. At the farther edge of the plain was a hill about one hundred and fifty feet high, the side towards us sloping at an angle of about forty degrees. On the top of the hill was a block-house and a structure that looked liked a shed. Here and there a puff of light smoke indicated that it was manned by infantry who were firing at us. I was at last where I had been trying to get—at the front. The hill was the position now so well known as the San Juan Hill. About one hundred yards in front of our main line, which I joined with my men, was a thin line of infantry firing at the enemy on the hill from behind a gentle swell in the ground.

I will now give the plan of battle as I deduce it from published reports and other literature of the campaign, and conversation with officers who participated in it. General Lawton, with his division and Capron's Battery, was to capture El Caney. This was to be accomplished by 8 or 9 A.M. In the mean time, Kent's division, and the cavalry division under Sumner, were to take position just beyond the San Juan River, the cavalry on the right of the road from El Pozo to

Santiago, the infantry on the left, and await orders. On the fall of El Caney, Lawton was to
turn to his left, executing a sort of grand left
wheel, and take position on the right of the cavalry, when orders were to issue for a general advance. It was four o'clock in the afternoon before Lawton succeeded in capturing El Caney,
and about noon on the following day when he
got into position on the right of the cavalry.
Now how did it happen that the attack on San
Juan was made about twenty-four hours earlier
than was contemplated in General Shafter's plan
of battle? The primary cause was that Kent's
and Sumner's divisions were ordered forward
prematurely.* They should not have moved beyond El Pozo until it was ascertained that Lawton had taken El Caney, and, once started, the
three divisions should have gone right on into
Santiago. Kent's division halted and deployed,
as ordered, on the line of the San Juan River, its
right resting on the road to Santiago. The cavalry division, under Sumner, deployed along the
Las Guamas Creek, its left resting on this road.
Both Kent and Sumner had received orders in
the morning from staff-officers of General Shafter
to halt on the edge of the woods, and these ended

* "After the battle of El Caney was well opened, the
sound of the small-arms' fire caused us to believe that
Lawton was driving the enemy before him." [General
Shafter's Report.]

about on the line formed by the San Juan River and Las Guamas Creek. General Shafter is doubtless in error in stating, as he does in his report, that General Sumner's orders of the morning required him to cross the San Juan River.

The position taken up as described, within decisive range of the enemy's infantry rifles, our artillery doing nothing to keep down his fire, was soon found to be untenable. Between 9 and 9.30 A.M., General Hawkins, commanding Kent's first brigade, and forming the right of the division, said to General Sumner, in the presence of General Kent, "We cannot stay here. It will not do for us to retire. The only alternative is to attack." And turning to his commander, he added, "If you will authorize it, General Kent, I will move my brigade around here against the enemy's right, and, with General Sumner co-operating, will engage to carry the enemy's position." Just then Lieutenant-Colonel Miley, General Shafter's chief of staff, came up, and General Hawkins made the proposition to him in the presence of Generals Kent and Sumner. It was about 10.30 A.M. when Lieutenant-Colonel Miley said, "General Kent, if you have no objection, I will order this movement in General Shafter's name." "Very well," said General Kent, who then rode off to hurry up the remainder of his division. Neither General

Wheeler nor General Shafter had anything to do with the initiation of the attack. It was subsequently to this informal council of war, the proceedings of which I have told as they were told to me by a member, that I joined Hawkins's brigade. The Sixth and Sixteenth Regulars were in position, waiting for the Seventy-first New York Volunteers, which Hawkins meant to place in rear of these regiments as a reserve. General Kent found the Seventy-first New York and started it forward, and also sent a note to Hawkins informing him of the fact; but neither the regiment nor the note ever reached its destination.

XIII

SAN JUAN

AT the point where we came upon it the road made a bend, the part to our right inclining towards the enemy's position at an angle of about forty-five degrees, that to our left being about parallel to it. The part to our right seemed to be raked by the enemy's fire, and I noticed a single officer walking up and down this road in rear of his men. From conversation with officers of the Sixteenth Infantry, I understand that this was Captain G. H. Palmer, of that regiment. I thought that I would do as he was doing, and then I thought I wouldn't. I compromised between standing up and lying down: I sat down. Soon afterwards Sergeant Elliot spoke up, and said, "Captain, you had better lie down, sir; it's pretty dangerous sitting up there." I thought the suggestion a good one, and lay down. The bullets were plunging into the road from the front as well as enfilading it from our right. Sergeant Elliot tells me that a man directly in rear of me was shot through the forehead, and that he has never been able to see how the bullet reached him without hitting me. I observed both here and in the road which I had crossed on my way to the front that there was no line of file-closers or officers in rear of the firing-line. The officers, non-commissioned officers, and privates were all in one line, practically shoulder to shoulder, and could be distinguished only by their uniforms. Sergeant Elliot asked my permission to go up to the fence and do some firing. I said, "Go ahead, Sergeant, if you think you can do any good." He accordingly stood up by the fence and fired seven shots, when, having attracted the enemy's fire, he fell back and lay down.

Along the side of the road in which we were lying ran a barbed-wire fence. I was soon cogitating as to how we should get through that fence when the time should come for us to advance. There was not a pair of wire-nippers in my troop. I understand, on good authority, that there were two hundred pairs on board our transport, the *Leona*. I wriggled myself up to one of the fence-posts and dug at the foot of it with both hands, but soon concluded that I could not accomplish anything in that way. I then stood up, and pulled and pushed at the post, but made no appreciable impression upon it. So I lay down again and left the fence alone.

It looked to me, while lying in this road, as if the advanced line to which I have referred fell back, but I am told that it did not. I asked the officer who was walking up and down in the road if it was not time for us to advance to its support. He replied that he supposed it would be pretty soon, or something to that effect, and went on walking as before. One man, who had no doubt been in the advance-line, fell back and halted directly in front of me in the tall grass on the opposite side of the fence. The silhouette of his manly young face and figure as he nestled up to the fence, his gun clutched in both hands, and his eyes riveted on the hill, are indelibly impressed upon my memory. I remarked to him that he had better come through the fence. Some one added, with true soldierly bluntness, "A man was shot there not long ago." He took a glance our way out of the corners of his eyes, and then replaced them upon the hill, seeming to close his fingers a little tighter, and so remained, as if hypnotized.

Suddenly my attention was attracted by a cry of pain, followed by moaning and groaning on my right. Turning my head, I saw a man sitting up holding his hand on his side. "Somebody take my gun," he said, "and blow my brains out. Won't somebody finish me? O, God! O, God!" He and Sergeant Elliot had been shooting at the hill. With the aid of Sergeant Elliot I examined his wound, as I thought. All that I found was an abrasion of two ribs. I told him that he was but slightly hurt. He said, " Oh, Captain, I can't breathe." I replied, " Yes, you can breathe, or you couldn't make so much noise. Now be quiet." He was quiet after that. I have since heard from Sergeant Elliot that this man was shot through the bowels, and have reproached myself for my impatience with him. He must have been wounded at least twice. Before long I was to know more than I did then about the sensations produced by Mauser bullets, and to have wounds of my own overlooked.

While gazing through the wire fence, I suddenly observed near the edge of the open field a swarm of men breaking forward from the direction of the road on my left. I jumped to my feet and, under the inspiration of the moment, took hold of the nearest fence-post, and put one foot on the lowest wire close to the post. Stepping from wire to wire as on the rounds of a ladder, I climbed to the top of the fence, and jumped from it down into the field, calling out as I struck the ground, " Come along, men !" After a momentary pause to see my men start through or over the fence, I struck out as fast as the tall grass would permit me towards the common objective of the mass of men which I now saw surging forward on my right and left. It was San Juan Hill, which Hawkins's brigade had undertaken to carry by assault. The cavalry division started forward, I believe, at the same time. In an account of the attack on San Juan Hill, by Richard Harding Davis, published in *Scribner's Magazine*, the writer does me the honor to mention me by name as one of the junior officers of the Tenth Cavalry who followed Colonel Roosevelt, as he, with his Rough Riders, broke cover and started across the plain. It is due to myself to say that whatever I did to contribute to the success of our arms was done without the inspiration of Colonel Roosevelt's example. It was never my good fortune to see that distinguished soldier in Cuba.

I had misgivings as to the result of our attempt. I thought of the Prussian Guards at St.-Privat, and almost expected that we would be brought to a halt and have to await reinforcements or supports before we reached the base of the hill. But we never stopped until we got to the top of it, excepting individual men who halted to fire over the heads of men and officers in front of them, and the unlucky ones, of whom I was one, who were arrested by Spanish bullets. We had advanced without any command that I know of, and the men commenced firing of their own accord. I tried to stop the firing, as I thought it would dangerously retard the advance, and other officers near me tried also to stop it. I even pointed my pistol at the men. But it was no use. A constant stream of bullets

went over the heads of the officers and of most
of the men towards the hill. The men covered
about fifty yards of ground from front to rear.
There was hardly a semblance of a line—simply
a broad swarm. The men cheered and yelled;
the officers, well out in front, where they belonged, waved their swords and showed them
the way. Some of the officers put their hats
on the points of their swords. I, not having
any sword or sabre, brandished my pistol. The
men kept up a double-time, except when they
halted to fire, which they did standing. I moved
at a run, but about every hundred yards threw
myself down in the grass to rest and allow the
men to close up on me. On my right, out in
front of everybody else, a stripling of a Cuban,
in the soiled white jacket and trousers common
both to Cubans and Spaniards, bounded forward,
waving his straw hat and occasionally looking back
at the troops. Our firing, though wild, was not
altogether ineffective, and retarded our advance
less than I at first thought it would. I could see
the side of the hill dotted with little clouds of
dust thrown up by our bullets. We peppered it
pretty hotly from top to bottom, and I have
learned since that many dead and wounded
Spaniards were found in the trenches on the top
of the hill. These casùalities, however, were
caused in part—perhaps mostly—by the fire of
our small advance-line before the assault. The

men in this line were, I believe, classified marks-
men and sharp-shooters.

As we approached the hill I asked an officer
near me whether he did not think we should try
to halt the men, and open a regular fire upon the
top of the hill. He replied to the effect that we
could not halt them, and that they might as well
keep a-going. So on we went. Just then, bang!
whiz! went a cannon-shot over our heads. Our
artillery had started shelling the top of the
hill. I wondered whether the artillery would
see us, and stop firing. A moment afterwards
it did stop, but, in the mean time, Captain Mc-
Farland, of the Sixteenth Infantry, among the
foremost on the hill, was struck in the back
of the head and disabled by a piece of shell.
When I was about half-way to the top my wind
completely gave out, and I threw myself down
for a moment's rest. On getting up, I stood
looking at the scene below me. About half a
mile across the bright green field, dotted here
and there with stately trees in which lurked the
reckless and murderous Spanish sharp-shooters,
stretched the on-coming shouting and shooting
mass of men in blue. A single banner of stars
and stripes, out-stretched by its cleaving of the
motionless air, fluttered proudly and inspiringly
over them, its shining spear seeming to point the
way forward and upward. I felt as if that human
billow would sweep away the enemy, hill and all,

and was never so proud of being an American as at that moment.

The enemy's position was about as nearly ideal as a real position can be. I have seen the famous stone wall at Fredericksburg backed by Marye's Heights. It is hardly a circumstance to this position. San Juan was more suggestive of Gettysburg than of Fredericksburg. Our attack seemed hardly less desperate than that of Pickett's division. At Gettysburg a cannonade of several hours' duration, designed to shake the *morale* of the defence, preceded the advance of the attacking infantry, which during this period of preparation was kept out of fire. At San Juan there was hardly any preparation by artillery, and the infantry and dismounted cavalry, who made the attack, were exposed to the enemy's fire for about an hour immediately preceding their advance, most of them not being able or permitted to fire back. I understand that it was not the commanding General's intention that San Juan should be attacked when it was. The troops, it seems, got out of his hands, which, as I have already intimated, was no more than I expected would happen the first time they should go into action. I am now satisfied that the Spaniards did not intend to make much of a stand at San Juan. It was only an outpost or advance position, and they began to retire from it, I believe, soon after our advance commenced, in order to establish themselves securely in their main position, which we never assailed. It is hardly fair to say that we drove them from San Juan. They gave us the position. If they had chosen to keep it, as I believe they had resolved to hold their main position in rear of it, we would at least have been checked, and might have been repulsed. As I was about to face to the front and go forward again, I felt as if my left leg were struck by a cannon-ball, the little finger of my left hand caught in a stone-crusher, and my right shoulder clawed by a wild-cat. I sat down and got out my first-aid package. Every officer and soldier carried a package of bandages for use in rendering first aid to the injured. In our regiment they were ordered to be kept in the left breast-pocket, so that they could be readily found by the surgeon.

XIV

WOUNDED

SERGEANT WILLIAM J. SCHUCK, of Company D, Sixth Infantry, came up to me and inquired if I was wounded. I replied that I was, and pointing to my left leg, said that I supposed I would have to lose it. He must have "been there" before, for he smiled as he answered, " It may not be so bad as that, Captain." With a pocket-knife he cut the leg of my trousers up to my knee, and found, in the fleshy part of the calf, two holes, where a bullet had gone in and come out. He called my attention to them and to the fact that they were not bleeding. I could hardly believe my eyes. I would not have been surprised if I had found the bulk of my leg from the knee down hanging by a shred, or discovered that it had been carried up the hill by the enemy's missile. I handed the Sergeant my first-aid package, remarking that it was not perfectly fresh. I had opened it out of curiosity, and to learn how to use it, before I landed in Cuba, not knowing that parts of the contents, being anti-septic, would be injured by exposure to the air.

The Sergeant took out his own package, and proceeded to dress my wounds with his bandages. I told him that he might need them himself, but he insisted upon using them. The bullet which went through my leg came from the direction of our men, or from my proper rear. It may have been sent by a Spanish sharp-shooter left behind by our advancing line, but was more probably the accidental or wild shot of one of our men. It may be that, as I rose from the ground facing our line, I was taken for a Spaniard. Many of our officers and men must have been in doubt or ignorance as to the uniform worn by the Spaniards, especially by the officers.

A number of my men came up to me inquiring if I was hurt, and offering to assist me. I told them that I was being attended to, and not to stop on my account, but to keep right on, that they were doing splendidly, and I was proud of them. My platoon went to the top of the hill with the infantry, and was afterwards conducted by an officer of the Tenth Cavalry to the line of the regiment a short distance to the right. In going up the San Juan Hill three of my men especially distinguished themselves; they were Sergeant James Elliot, Corporal John Walker, and Private (now Corporal) Luchious Smith. Sergeant Elliot and Private Smith were, during the ascent of the hill, constantly among the bolder few who voluntarily made themselves ground - scouts, drawing the attention of the enemy from the main line upon themselves. Corporal Walker was with the handful of fearless spirits who accompanied Lieutenant J. G. Ord, of the Sixth U. S. Infantry, forming, with that splendid young soldier, the point of General Hawkins's gallant brigade, the head and front of the assault. Following is Corporal Walker's own story, told under oath:

STATE OF ALABAMA, }
COUNTY OF MADISON. } *ss.*

Personally appeared before me, the undersigned, Corporal John Walker, Troop D, Tenth Cavalry, who, being duly sworn according to law, deposes and says that on the 1st of July, 1898, he was engaged in the assault on San Juan Hill, at a point where there was a block-house, a shed, and a line of intrenchments; that just before the foremost assailants reached the foot of the hill our artillery commenced firing over the assailants at the enemy on the top of the hill; that when the deponent was about half-way up the hill, the only persons near him, except an officer who was disabled, were Lieutenant Ord, of the Sixth U. S. Infantry, and Private (now Corporal) Luchious Smith, Troop D, Tenth Cavalry; that the main line was about fifty yards in rear of this party, with a light scattering of men between it and this party; that the said Lieutenant Ord, evidently observing that our artillery fire had caused a slowing up in the main line, called out in a loud tone, looking towards the main line and waving his hat, " Come on, men,

we've got them on the go!" having repeatedly before
urged the men on with voice and gesture; that the deponent reached the intrenchments about fifty yards in
advance of the main line; that the only persons near
him at that time were the said Lieutenant Ord, a private
of the Sixth U. S. Infantry, and a private of the Sixteenth U. S. Infantry; that about twenty yards to his
left and about on a line with him was the said Private
Luchious Smith; that about twenty-five yards in rear of
the deponent was a scattering of other soldiers, foremost among whom was Sergeant James Elliot, Troop
D, Tenth Cavalry; that the deponent found two Spaniards alive and a number dead and wounded in the intrenchments; that the two former threw up their hands
and surrendered; that the deponent took from one of
them a pearl-handled pistol and gave it to the said Lieutenant Ord; that the Lieutenant said, " Let us go to
this block - house and capture these men in it"; that
having gone about four yards in the direction of the
block-house the Lieutenant stopped behind a tree, and,
leaning to one side, looked in the direction of the retreating enemy; that as he did so, he was shot with a
pistol directly under the chin by a Spaniard on the other
side of the tree; that as he fell at the Corporal's feet, he
said, " If we had the rest of the Tenth Cavalry here,
we could capture this whole command"; that the Lieutenant died about five minutes afterwards, or about ten
minutes after he was shot; that the man who shot him
ran off; that the deponent fired at him twice, and saw
him fall; that he and the forementioned private of the
Sixteenth U. S. Infantry examined the man who had
shot Lieutenant Ord immediately after the Corporal had
fired at him, and found that he was shot through the
body twice, both shots going through the small of the
back; that he was apparently dead, and that he, the de-

ponent, is satisfied that the man in question was killed by him, the deponent.

Further deponent sayeth not.

JOHN WALKER,
Corporal Troop D, Tenth Cavalry.

Sworn to and subscribed before me, at Camp A. G. Forse, Huntsville, Alabama, this 19th day of December, 1898.
S. D. FREEMAN,
First Lieutenant, Tenth Cavalry.
Judge Advocate, General Court-Martial.

First Sergeant W. H. Givens was ever at his post exercising a steadying or encouraging influence upon the men, and conducting himself like the thorough soldier which I have long known him to be.

I took into action, including Lieutenant Kennington's platoon, but not including the two men left to guard the packs, two (2) officers and forty-eight (48) men. My losses were as follows:

Killed: Private George Stovall.

Wounded: Captain John Bigelow, Jr., Sergeant George Dyals, Sergeant Willis Hatcher, Privates J. H. Campbell, Henry Fearn, Fred Shockley, Harry Sturgis, James F. Taylor.

Missing: Private James Clay.

After Sergeant Schuck had dressed my leg and little finger, I got up and stood for some time watching troops rushing across the plain, some in lines and swarms, some in long, thin columns. Ob-

serving that the firing seemed to be growing hot-
ter on my right, as I stood facing to the rear, and
hearing some one near me say that our men were
having a hot time on the right, I called out towards the left that troops were needed on the right,
and saw several regiments go streaking off in that
direction. As I hobbled off to the rear, accompanied by a wounded infantryman, and leaning
on his gun, I looked around for litter-bearers.
Some years before, while serving at a frontier
post, I attended a lecture, given by a medical officer, on the care of wounded in battle. On the
strength of what I there heard, I told my com-
panion that we would soon come upon first-aid
stations, and find Red Cross flags on posts and
trees, indicating the way to a division hospital.
As we started from the foot of the hill, across the
plain, a medical officer, probably a regimental
surgeon, came running up to us from a column
on our left, and asked if there was anything he
could do for us. I said I thought not, as our
wounds had been dressed, and he hastened back
to his post. Bullets flew thick and fast over
our heads, but at a safe distance. Thinking we
could make better time on a road than in the
tall grass of the plain, we inclined to our left and
got into the road in which we had lain, about
midway between San Juan Hill and where I had
myself lain with my men. I frequently stopped
and looked back at the hill. From the road I saw

our Gatling guns, the men and pieces standing
out against the sky on a spur of the hill sloping
off to the right as I faced the hill, the pieces
pointing towards the left, their steady, monoto-
nous grindings contrasting with the gusts and
squalls of our musketry. Here and there along
the side of the hill, under cover of its crest, stood
a group of mounted officers.

As I went on down the road I passed a number of corpses lying with their faces up, covered
with pieces of blanket. Coming to the place
where I had lain, I found the man whom I had
examined when he was shot, lying on his back,
his head propped up, looking pretty comfortable.
Not far beyond him I caught the glazed, staring
eyes of a man reclining on a low bank by the
side of the road with a pool of clotted blood in
his open mouth. I had been joined by this time
by Private Boarman, of my troop, whom the First
Sergeant had sent to look after me. My first
impulse was to send him back to the troop, but,
appreciating the motive of First Sergeant Givens,
and the man's evident feeling for me, I had not
the heart to do it.

The bullets were passing pretty close to the
ground. At the suggestion of the men who were
with me, I lay down in the road and waited for
them to hunt around for a dressing-station or
field-hospital. They did not find any, but the
infantryman had found a place where wounded

men were being gathered together. It was in a
belt of trees between a creek and the plain over
which we had charged, at the point where a road
crossed the creek. I believe it has been called
The Bloody Ford. A line-officer had gotten a
few able-bodied men together, and had them
gather the long grass and make a sort of bed of
it under cover of a slight embankment. A number of wounded officers and men lay stretched
out on this bed. A large camp-fire blazed near
by. While I lay here bullets whistled through
the foliage overhead and the woods across the
creek. The din of battle, growing now fainter,
now louder, kept us constantly interested in the
situation at the front. Every little while a
wounded man would raise himself so as to see
over the embankment, and take a look at San
Juan Hill. One poor fellow, while doing so, fell
back with a groan, mortally wounded. There was
no surgeon or nurse present. Wounded men
kept coming in and lying down with us, or strid-
ing across the creek to make their way to the
Division Hospital. Now and then the body of a
dead officer would be laid down in front of us.
But I do not remember seeing a man brought in
or go by on a regular litter. The wounded, as I
remember, carried themselves or were carried by
other men, either on their backs or on improvised litters, made with guns or poles and blankets or articles of clothing. When I last com-

manded a troop at an army-post, troop and company commanders were required to have four men constantly under training at the post hospital as litter-bearers. These men had to be excused from military drill, stables, or anything else that would interfere with this training. I entertained the belief that if I ever saw a battle I should experience or witness a practical application of the most approved methods of litter-bearing on an adequate scale.

XV

IN DIVISION HOSPITAL

LATE in the afternoon an ambulance arrived. The surgeon in charge of it picked out the more serious cases, including me among them. My old friend Ducat, of the Twenty-fourth, with a wound in the abdomen, was laid on his back in the bottom of the vehicle. Another officer was stretched out on one of the seats, his head resting in the lap of the surgeon. On the same seat with me sat Captain Fornance, of the Thirteenth Infantry, with a mortal wound through the body. As we were slowly drawn over the rough road to the Division Hospital, about two miles distant, I was moved with sympathy and admiration for the wounded men I saw trudging along. There was nothing on wheels to carry them, not even an army wagon. The road seemed lined for some distance with men of the Seventy-first New York, who did not look as if they had been near a fight.

We reached the hospital after dark. I was the first to get out of the ambulance. As I hobbled up to one of the operating-tents the table, covered with white oil-cloth, was being sponged off. The sponge was thrown into a bucket of bloody water, the surgeon called " Next," and I stepped in. With the assistance of an attendant I laid myself out on the table. After my leg and finger had been dressed, the surgeon was about to have me helped down. I remarked that I believed that I was hurt in the shoulder. He examined me there, and replied, "I should say you were." This was a surface wound, a furrow, not unlike a cut. It was soon dressed, and I made room for the next subject. I was agreeably surprised in getting off without the loss of my little finger, the bone of which was shattered, for I was prepared to submit to its amputation. The ground about the tent was strewn with wounded men lying on it, among whom other men, mostly wounded, were moving or standing. I lay down on the grass, and tried to go to sleep. I had not eaten anything since breakfast, and had no blanket or overcoat. On the way to the hospital I had looked out for the packs of my troop, but in the dusk and darkness I could not recognize them. Private Boarman, whom I had sent to look for my pack, sent me word that he had not been able to find it. I had quite resigned myself to a night of discomfort, if not of suffering, when I was asked by a soldier standing over me if he could not do something for me. I told him that I did not think he could. On learning from me that I had nothing to eat, he asked me if I would not like something. I said I would. He then told me that he could get me some coffee, bacon, hard-tack, and canned tomatoes. I declined the coffee, but accepted the rest. With my approval, he prepared the hard - tack as soldiers commonly do, by soaking it in water and frying it in bacon grease. While I was eating this supper he learned from me that I had no covering, and at once proposed to get me a blanket. I said, "You have but one blanket, and need it as much as I." He answered, "I bunk with other men, sir, and their blankets will do for me," and went and got his blanket and put it over me. I had hardly turned over after this to go to sleep when I felt a touch on my shoulder, and, looking up, saw a hospital-corps man, who said that he recognized me as an officer and that there was a place provided under cover for wounded officers. I went with him to a litter under a tent-fly, where I lay down among other wounded officers. I passed a comfortable night, except that I was disturbed once or twice by other patients calling for the attendant. The latter was a soldier. He was constantly under the fly or near by, and always prompt in answering calls. While the officers were thus provided for, the men had to shift for themselves. I understand that most of the wounded soldiers spent the night under the open sky, without blankets, and with nothing to eat.

IN DIVISION HOSPITAL

Early in the morning the man who had furnished me supper and a blanket came to see how I was, and asked what I would like for breakfast. I took everything that he had to give me, which was what he had offered me for supper—including the coffee. When I had finished breakfast, he asked what I would like for lunch, and when he should bring it. I thanked him, and told him that I hoped to be out of that hospital by lunch-time, and that if I was not I would trust to the hospital for nourishment. I wanted to return his blanket, but he insisted upon my keeping it. I promised to send it back to him from Siboney, where I expected to go. I had taken his name, troop, and regiment the evening before, and regret very much that I have lost my memorandum. If I remember rightly, he was a private in Troop D of the First Cavalry, camped as a guard near the hospital. The food that he brought me was part of his own ration.

XVI

IN GENERAL HOSPITAL

EARLY in the day I applied to the surgeon in charge to be sent down to Siboney, with a view to being shipped to the United States. I was informed that there was nothing but army wagons to move the wounded in, and that if I could stand the trip, I might be sent down in the afternoon, that during the forenoon only men who could stand up would be moved. I got off that afternoon in the first wagon that carried men lying down. The bottom of the wagon was covered with a layer of grass about thick enough to hide the planks, but not to form much of a cushion. An army wagon, be it known, has no springs. My companions were mostly officers. Although we travelled at a walk, the jarring and jolting kept us bracing ourselves and gritting our teeth for the nine miles or more that we had to get over. We passed many wounded men making their way on foot. At the suggestion of Captain Rodman, of the Twentieth Infantry, sitting next to me, we stopped and, crowding ourselves a little closer, took in one of them. "A noble

fellow," the Captain said, belonging to his company. Before we got to the end of our ride
that soldier got us to stop and let him out. He
preferred to walk.

Siboney seemed to consist chiefly of a row of
houses facing the beach, about two hundred
yards from the water. The principal, if not only,
street ran in front of these houses. The hospital
consisted of a row of "hospital" tents facing
these houses and the beach, for they were open
at both ends. They stood in pairs, back to back,
and opening into each other. We were placed
in a tent next to the street, each on a wire cot,
without mattress. The nights were quite cool,
and with but one blanket I should have slept
better on the ground than on the cot. But I
succeeded in getting another blanket from the
hospital. I spent a good deal of my time here
looking out on the street from my cot. The
houses, I was told, were formerly used by the
Spaniards as barracks. At present they were occupied by Cuban families. They have since been
burned as a precaution against yellow-fever.
They all had narrow porches on the street, and
on these porches men and women were taking
their ease, and children playing, all day long.
The street was always alive with soldiers and
citizens, wagons, ambulances, pack-trains, etc.
The most interesting sight that presented itself
to me was a batch of Spanish prisoners—I be-

lieve they were taken at El Caney—escorted by
a troop of our mounted cavalry, armed with carbine, sabre, and pistol. The people in the street
stood still, and those in the houses came out on
the porches. It was the first and only time
during the campaign that I saw a Spanish soldier.
I should not have known these from Cubans if I
had seen them by themselves. Like Cubans,
they were small, lightly built men. They marched
at a good gait, keeping up with the long-legged
horses of their escort, who seemed to be making
from three to four miles an hour. They bore
themselves, I thought, with true Spanish dignity,
holding their heads high even when glancing to
right or left at the staring crowd. Cuban women
hung over the railings of the porches pointing and
jeering at them. The Cuban men watched them
with comparative gravity. About the middle of
the column a couple of prisoners bore on their
shoulders the ends of a hammock in which a
human figure lay coiled up. "Poor fellow," I
thought, "how much better off I am than you!"
But I have something to say about my trials.

Nobody came to me here to give me a soldier's ration. By evening, having had no lunch,
I was pretty hungry. What food and drink I
got here was brought or sent to the officers by
Chaplain Bateman, or another chaplain whose
name I did not learn. These two gentlemen
worked heroically, ministering to the wants of

the sick and wounded. No men who took part in the campaign are worthier of recognition for faithful and meritorious services than they are. But to speak for myself: I felt the pangs of hunger. One of the surgeons or civilian doctors told me that there were no rations to feed us on but those furnished for the hospital-corps. The Commissary Officer, when I quoted this to him, said that there was an abundance of rations within a stone's-throw of the hospital, and that the medical department could have all that it wanted of them on requisition. There was no nurse or other attendant in our tent. The sink, I was told, was several hundred yards away. There was no earth closet, and, so far as I could learn, no vessel to use in lieu of one. I remember our getting one or two persons to hunt around for accommodations of this sort, and receiving from them an old tomato-can and a stone crock, which they had picked up outside of the hospital. We had generally to wait on ourselves, or watch for an opportunity to call in a passing soldier or civilian to render us such service as we needed. Red Cross nurses, with their neat white caps and aprons, flitting past our tent, made the situation the more trying. They seemed busy, and, I suppose, could not attend to us.

In the evening I had my wounds dressed again. When my little finger was laid bare, the attendant remarked to the surgeon, " I suppose that will have to come off, sir?" The surgeon replied, " No, I think we can save that finger; the Captain, I suppose, would rather have a stiff finger than none at all." I am grateful to that surgeon, though I sometimes think the finger in question would not have been very much of a loss. After the three wounds which had been dressed before had been attended to, I raised myself to get off the table, and as I did so felt a sort of itching in my left thigh. I remarked to the surgeon that something made me feel as if I had been hit there. He examined the place and found a bullet-hole. He then looked for another, and not finding it, concluded that the bullet was still in me. He would not probe for it, he said, but when I got North I should have it located by means of the X-rays and cut out.

XVII

VERY soon after arriving in the hospital at Siboney, I made application to be sent on board the *Olivette*, which I thought was about to return to the United States. I was promised that my wish should be gratified. In anticipation of my departure, I procured from the Commissary several cans of peaches and meat, a pipe and a pound of tobacco, did them up in the blanket belonging to the soldier who had shared his rations with me at the Division Hospital, and gave the package to a teamster to deliver or have delivered for me to the soldier. I have never heard whether they ever reached their destination.

I have before me bits of paper on which are scratched the messages that passed on the following day (July 3d) between Major La Garde, surgeon in charge, and myself, on the ways and means of getting me aboard ship. I trust that I am not betraying confidence in presenting this informal correspondence to the reader.

SANTIAGO CAMPAIGN

CAPTAIN BIGELOW,—You can be transferred to the *Olivette* — you and Captain Ducat — by going to the landing. Let me know what transportation you require.   L. A. L.

DEAR MAJOR,—We shall each require a litter with four men—so that the bearers can be relieved. Sincerely,
                                                      J. BIGELOW, JR.

I am having a travois made; it will be ready in two hours.   LA GARDE.

[Two or three hours later.]

DEAR DOCTOR, — The travois has not come. Sincerely,   J. BIGELOW, JR.

Travois is ready. Great confusion. Transfer of wounded to boats very slow. Wait!   LA GARDE.

I waited. When a medical officer, on his round that afternoon, asked me whether my wounds had been dressed since the night before, I replied that they had not, but that I expected to have them dressed on the " Hospital Ship." Late in the afternoon I was hauled in a travois to the landing. A number of officers and men were waiting to be taken off. Something, I believe, was being done to the landing. At any rate, I lay here on a litter about an hour. I was informed by a medical officer at the landing that the vessel that I was to go on was not the *Olivette*, but the *Cherokee*. I showed my message from Major La Garde, but it made no difference. The *Olivette*, I understood afterwards, was full, and was not to go to the United States, but to remain as a floating hospital at Siboney.

At last Chaplain Bateman, who was conducting the embarkation, sent word that he was ready for me. A small boat touched at the landing, and a throng of men pushed towards it. Above the shuffling and clattering of feet came the Chaplain's organ voice, " Stand back, men ! This is a special boat for Captain Bigelow. No one else is to get in it." The sound of feet died away. The men ranged themselves on both sides of the pier, and the litter on which I lay went down the aisle to the boat, which was bobbing up and down and bumping against the dock. The litter, with me on it, was passed to the men in the boat, who laid it on the seats, the boat pushed off, and I was rowed out about a quarter of a mile to the *Cherokee*, where the boat, with crew and all, was hoisted to the top of the rail, the litter handed over to men on deck, and I was carried into the saloon. I was given a bowl of soup and a bread-and-butter sandwich, the best thing that I had eaten since I left the *Leona*, but not by any means enough to satisfy me. I soon found out that the *Cherokee* was a hospital ship only in name.

My wounds were not dressed that day. The next day, July 4th, we remained at anchor, taking sick and wounded aboard. This day my wounds were dressed by a surgeon, Major Heil, of the Regular Army, who was not fit for duty, being himself on the sick report. He found another hole in my thigh, establishing the fact that the bullet which had gone in at one place had come out at another.

I was clothed in the uniform and underclothing in which I had been wounded, and had no change for either. Most of the officers and men were in the same fix. There was no apparent relief for the men. But most, if not all, of the officers had underclothing among their possessions on the transports that had brought them to Cuba. These vessels were riding at anchor within sight, and many of them within hailing distance of us. We tried to have our trunks, valises, rolls of bedding, etc., brought or sent to us, but it apparently could not be done. At any rate it was not done, except in a very few cases. Fortunately for me, my old friend—old in friendship — Major Coe, of the Regular Infantry, was aboard, and was one of the few officers who had gotten hold of his personal baggage. He had a suit of underclothing which he said he wanted me to wear, and I took him at his word.

There was no ice aboard. It appears that the Quartermaster, who should have seen to the supply, never inspected the vessel nor made any inquiry of the Captain, nor sent him any instructions regarding it.

On the following day, July 5th, we weighed anchor and steamed away for the United States. In the mean time a surgeon, Major Rafferty, of the U. S. Army, had come aboard and taken charge of the sick and wounded officers and soldiers, numbering about three hundred. He was assisted by a few hospital-corps men, but they had practically no time for nursing. There was no Red Cross nurse aboard. The demand for crutches was partially met by the mate, who made a number out of ship's lumber.

The men had regular rations, cooked at the ship's galley. The officers ate, as they had done coming to Cuba, in the saloon, paying at the same rate, fifty cents a meal. The fare was poorer and slimmer than on the way out. I had taken only two meals at the passengers' table when I had an unpleasantness with a waiter, which wound up with my uttering an imprecation on his whole set, and announcing and resolving that I would never take another meal served by any of them. A number of officers besides myself were satisfied that they could fare better for less money by rustling than by patronizing the steward. We united ourselves into a mess, which flourished during the remainder of the voyage. How we got our victuals need not be told. Suffice it to say that our method would not have worked if we had not kept on good terms with the military cook.

One night I was awakened by a succession of loud reports, which I immediately recognized as cannon-shots. Accompanying these sounds was a great shuffling of feet and confusion of voices. " Why the —— don't our ship stop?" said one. " It is stopping," said another. " I'm —— if it is." Bang! whiz! The shuffling of feet seemed to increase. I thought of getting up, but at once perceived the uselessness of my doing so. If I was going to drown, I might as well lie in my warm bed as long as I could. Our vessel slackened her speed and stopped. Presently I heard the splashing of another close by and a voice, "What ship is this?" " The *Cherokee*." " Why haven't you got your lights out?" I do not remember the answer, but the facts were that the Captain did not know enough. The vessel hailing us was a gunboat on the lookout for Spanish blockade-runners. Seeing us going along without any lights, it took us for a Spaniard and fired across our bow. Our Captain, instead of coming to, tried to run away. As a consequence we came near being sent to the bottom. Our officers answered a few questions about the situation in Cuba, and we started off. We had not gone far before we were hailed with a cannon-shot again. The necessary lights had not been shown. With the information obtained from a foreign naval officer on board of our vessel as a passenger, somebody posted our Captain as to the lights required on a hospital ship—a white light at the masthead, in addition to the usual lights, which, I believe, are a red and a green one at the sides, and a white one at the bow. There was no Red Cross flag on our vessel. The officers talked some of making one, but gave it up as impracticable or as unnecessary, considering the crippled condition of the enemy's fleet.

We expected to land at Key West, but on the night of the 8th, as we approached that point, we were hailed by a war-vessel and notified that we were to go on to Tampa, where a hospital-train would be awaiting us to take us North. We cheerfully resigned ourselves to another night aboard ship, with the prospect of going North on landing. We reached Tampa after dark. I was not surprised to learn that the train was not ready for us. We waited several hours at the dock before landing. The train remained near the transport, where we boarded it, and there it remained until the next morning. It then moved a few miles—to Tampa, if I remember rightly. It was not until after noon that it started for its destination, McPherson Barracks, near Atlanta, Georgia. We were more comfortable than we had been on the water. Each officer and man had a berth in a tourist, or emigrant, car. In the officers' car, and I suppose in each of the other cars, were a couple of men of the hospital corps, acting as nurses. Substantial meals were served in a dining-car, and we did not have to pay for them. At the stations we were the object of considerable interest to the people there assembled, but we did not come in for any of the organized relief that we had heard and read about. At one station, however, a lady sent to her house for a quantity of milk, which she gave to officers and men.

There was one incident of our journey which I think pretty well matched the one on the water which I have told of. It was evening; our train came to a stop, we knew not why. Suddenly we heard a loud report, which I suspected was a torpedo on the track. We looked at one another. Some one jestingly remarked, "Another cannonade." He had hardly spoken when a terrible crash was heard at the rear end of the train ; our car seemed to jump about fifty yards, and went tearing down the track to the accompaniment of crashing at the rear. I was seated facing the rear, and kept my seat. An officer with his arm in a sling, who was standing facing me, was thrown against the back of a seat and given a pretty sharp twinge. I do not know of any of the officers or men being badly hurt, but they were all more or less shaken physically, if not morally. We wondered what was going to happen next, and what our chances were of reaching Fort McPherson. Some of the officers went to the rear of the train, where they saw a mound of débris, the wreck of the caboose, completely hiding the engine of the train which had run into us. That train, I was told, was an express, going at the rate of sixty miles an hour. However, we did get safely to Fort McPherson, arriving there on the 12th. When the surgeon examined me, which he did the following day, he found my wounds suppurating, and my temperature 105 degrees. My wounds, with the exception of my little finger, had not been dressed since the 4th, eight long and tedious days.

XVIII

CONVALESCENCE

THANKS to the skilful treatment of Major Blair D. Taylor, U. S. Army, Post Surgeon at Fort McPherson, and the excellent nursing of a young lady who had volunteered for her noble work, I was cured of fever in less than six days, and two days later, July 20th, was allowed to leave the hospital. Major Taylor kindly applied to the War Department to have the sick and wounded officers ordered to their homes to await further orders. This would have given us mileage for the distances travelled. But we were simply given leaves of absence, which left us to pay our own travelling expenses.

After spending a few weeks in Baltimore, where I had the splinters of my shattered finger extracted by a civilian doctor, I went to the Catskill Mountains to gain strength. It was not many weeks before I weighed more than I did when I went to the war. I could not help feeling a little selfish when I read of the horrors of the early days at Camp Wikoff, and thought of the comfort and attention which I enjoyed. While convalescing, I received my back mail. One letter, mailed and registered in Boston on the 15th of June, was delivered to me on the 15th of September.

My leave extended to the 20th of September. In order not to have to make the journey back to Fort McPherson at my own expense, I applied to the War Department about the 1st of September for orders returning me to duty. About the middle of the month I received an order directing me to proceed to Camp Wikoff, Montauk Point, and join my regiment.

XIX

RETURN TO DUTY

EN ROUTE to Camp Wikoff, I stopped at Highland Falls, near West Point, to visit my father, and while there was warned by an army friend against the dampness of Montauk Point as likely to irritate my wounds. Understanding that my regiment was about to leave Montauk for the South, I saw the post surgeon at West Point, and procured through him an extension of my leave, which I spent at Highland Falls. In the mean time my regiment was moved to Huntsville, Alabama. I wrote to the Adjutant-General for another order, assuming that the last one ceased to be operative upon the departure of my regiment from Montauk. I was informed in reply that no other order was necessary, that the order which I had, together with paragraph 1330 of the Army Regulations, required me to join my regiment wherever it might be, and would secure me mileage. On the expiration of my extension I proceeded to Huntsville, and joined my regiment at Camp Wheeler, named after General Wheeler, commanded by General Wheeler, and

in General Wheeler's congressional district. The
name has since been changed to Camp A. G.
Forse, after Major Forse, of the First U. S. Cavalry, killed at San Juan. I sent my mileage
accounts to the Paymaster - General. After a
while they came back with an indorsement to
the effect that to secure mileage I must have
an order directing me to proceed to Huntsville,
Alabama. I promptly forwarded the papers
to the Adjutant - General, but have not heard
from him, and am still waiting for my mileage
(December 19, 1898).

In all directions around the city of Huntsville
are scattered camps of the regiments and batteries
of the Fourth Army Corps. There have been
some heavy frosts, and one morning I found the
water in my bucket covered with a sheet of ice.*
It rains more than it shines, and blows a good
deal. My regiment is camped in a field of pure
clay, which had been under cultivation. The
only green things on it now are weeds and recruits. When it rains we go slipping and flounder-
ing around, between our tents and picket-lines,
with several pounds of mud hanging to our
rubber boots—those of us who are fortunate
enough to possess such foot-gear. The Government does not furnish rubber boots or rubber

* Since writing the above it has taken to freezing every
night.

overcoats, nor keep them for sale. Most of the
men and officers have provided themselves with
them at their own expense. The men are in
what are called common wall-tents, three in a tent.
The floors are just wide enough for three beds to
lie on them side by side. There are no stoves
for these tents. I have had a rude high table
constructed near the cook-fire, where the men
eat standing in the open air.* Thanks to the
prosperity of our Exchange (canteen), which may
be mainly attributed to the businesss ability and
energy of its present manager, Lieutenant Dixon,
I have a good company fund, and so am able to
give the men as substantial and palatable a diet
as soldiers have any right to expect. To save
the cook, the Quartermaster-Sergeant, and myself from having to think from day to day and
meal to meal what to cook or have cooked, I

---

* I had hardly penned the above lines when an orderly
handed me the following communication:

Circular.   HEADQUARTERS TENTH CAVALRY,
                                November 16, 1898.

Troop commanders will designate the place where their troop
kitchens and dining-rooms are to be built, as nearly as possible
on a continuation of the line of their troop tents.

    *   *   *   *   *   *   *

                                        S. J. WOODWARD,
                               Captain Tenth Cavalry, Com'd'g.

These buildings were hardly put up and fitted out
when the regiment was moved to Texas.

have drawn up the bill of fare that appears below. It is not " cast-iron." I occasionally add to it or change it; but it is never departed from without my knowledge and approval. The coffee is sweetened, but there is no milk to go with it.

BILL OF FARE OF TROOP D, TENTH CAVALRY

	Breakfast.	Dinner.	Supper.
Sunday	Beef, gravy. oatmeal, milk, coffee, bread.	Rice, beans, baked tomatoes, bread, duff.	Stewed beef, onions, apples, coffee, bread.
Monday	Beefsteak, coffee, bread.	Roast beef, gravy, rice, sweet-potatoes, bread.	Stewed beef, baked sweet-potatoes, coffee, bread.
Tuesday	Beef stew, coffee, bread.	Roast beef, gravy, mashed potatoes, stewed tomatoes, bread.	Beef, Irish potatoes, stewed apples, coffee, bread.
Wed'day	Fried bacon, gravy, coffee, bread.	Roast beef, gravy, sweet-potatoes, cabbage, bread.	Baked salmon, syrup, coffee, corn-bread.
Thur'day	Beefsteak, oatmeal, milk, coffee, bread.	Stewed beef, Irish potatoes, onions, bread.	Baked potatoes, beef, gravy, coffee, bread.
Friday	Beef, gravy, sweet-potatoes, coffee, bread.	Beans, bacon, tomato soup, onions, bread.	Beef, potatoes, onions, coffee, bread.
Saturday	Roast beef, baked sweet-potatoes, coffee, bread.	Stewed beef, cabbage, bacon, bread.	Irish potatoes, fried bacon, syrup, coffee, corn-bread.

The accommodations of the officers are luxuri-
ous compared to those of the men. Each has at
least one regular wall-tent, and most of them
have two or three, owing to the absence of many
officers. They have provided themselves with
heating-stoves at their own expense. The Quartermaster furnished cooking-stoves, but did not
have enough to go around. I had to buy both of
my stoves, and the pipes and zinc for them.

I believe all the camps except ours had some
protection from the wind. Ours got the four
winds of heaven in turn, if not in combination. I
had hoped that the War Investigating Commission
would visit our camp on a rainy day. When it
came to Huntsville I was at Philadelphia, with
a detachment of the regiment, attending the
Peace Jubilee parade. The Commissioners did
not come out to the camp nor see any officer on
duty with the regiment.

On the 16th of October, the day of my arrival
in camp, my morning report showed eighty-three
men present and forty-eight horses, about one
horse for every two men. About fifty per cent. of
the men were recruits. The horses were a sorry
lot. Many of them never had looked well, but
they now looked pitiable. I have been told that
they were terribly worried by the flies at Lakeland, where they were kept during the campaign
tied to a picket-line. There was no paddock or
corral to turn them loose in, and the men avail-

able for grooming and feeding them were mostly recruits. It will be remembered that many of these horses were received at Lakeland just as we were preparing to take the field, with all the trained men of two squadrons *dismounted*. The recruits were kept regularly drilling and target-firing, in addition to attending, together with the older men, to the horses of the regiment.

I learned in our present camp that First Sergeant Givens had been commissioned as Second Lieutenant in an immune regiment. I found Sergeant Elliot acting as First Sergeant, and appointed him to that position. I have recommended him and Corporal Smith for a certificate of merit, which brings two dollars of extra pay a month, and Corporal Walker for a medal of honor. Private Boarman, on returning to the troop in front of Santiago, had three ribs broken by the roof of a bomb-proof falling in on him. At his request I have applied for his discharge on account of physical disability. I have several men on light duty by reason of wounds from which they have not yet recovered. I found the troop without nose-bags or feed-boxes. The grain fed to the horses was dropped on the ground at their feet, which is ordinarily wet or muddy. Of course a good deal of the grain was lost. The horses were practically not receiving their allowance of it. After a while I was equipped with nose-bags. But soon after

163

that the number of my horses was increased to about two-thirds the number needed, and this left me again short of nose-bags. A number of my men are in need of gloves, overcoats, and other articles of clothing, which our Quartermaster has either not at all, or not of the sizes to fit them.

The routine of camp-life is about the same as it was at Chickamauga and at Lakeland. There is no exercising in large bodies. I understand that our regiment is brigaded with certain other regiments, but what regiments these are, where their camps are, and who commands the brigade, I have forgotten, if I ever knew. In our regiment the drilling is confined to troop drill and squad drill, the latter for recruits. The proportion of recruits, I understand, is large in all the regiments. Few of the enlisted men whom I pass on the streets of Huntsville salute me: I do not know why, unless it is that they are not in the habit of saluting their officers.

XX

CONCLUSION

BEFORE the fall of Santiago the promotion of officers especially commended to the War Department and the consequent overslaughing of others was inaugurated. At the battle of San Juan the commanders of the First and Tenth U. S. Cavalry, whose services dated respectively from 1861 and 1862, were under the orders of a young man who entered the army in 1886, and at the beginning of the war was an assistant surgeon with the rank of captain. Upon the close of the campaign and the return of the troops to the United States, it seemed as if everybody who could be made a brigadier-general was. For those who were not deemed worthy of such promotion, or some other, the only hope of reward lay in the brevet appointments which the War Department was preparing to recommend to the President. A brevet commission does not confer any rank nor carry any pay with it. A brevet is practically an empty title. The recommendations were made, but could not be acted on because they required the approval of the Senate, and that methodical body would not delay its adjournment long enough to consider them.

For the soldiers, one immediate effect of the declaration of peace was a twenty per cent. reduction of their pay, which had been increased in that proportion for the war. A simultaneous hardship which they felt perhaps as much as this one, but which fortunately proved to be but temporary, was their deprivation of beer and light wines at post-canteens. The reader may need to be informed that the post-canteen is a soldiers' club under the general management of an officer. It is intended, like the club to which, say, the reader belongs, to provide innocent amusement and harmless refreshment. It is a place in which a soldier can go after dark and have a sociable pipe and glass of beer or wine, and take a hand at pool, poker, ninepins, or other game, without having to fight the temptations of rot-gut whiskey and painted women. Some well-meaning, but misguided, philanthropists had a law enacted which was intended apparently to prohibit the sale of beer and light wines on military reservations. But, as construed by the Attorney-General, its only effect is to prohibit such sale *by officers or soldiers*.

Some of the men who had accepted commissions in volunteer regiments had, after the war, to go back to the ranks. When the regiment in which First Sergeant Givens, of my troop, was commissioned was mustered out, he returned to duty with the Tenth Cavalry; but in the mean time he had lost his position as First Sergeant. At last accounts he was serving as Corporal in the troop of which he was First Sergeant before the war.*

Men recommended for medals of honor and certificates of merit will, like the officers recommended for brevets, have to wait for them until the next session of Congress, if not longer. In the mean time a number of them will have died of new wounds and disease, if not of their old ones. But who says that our country is ungrateful to " the man behind the gun ?"

Sound tactics and strategy depend upon the observance of three cardinal unities :

1. Unity of purpose.
2. Unity of command.
3. Unity of mass, or concentration of forces.

In the Santiago campaign there were two distinct purposes, the destruction or capture of Cervera's fleet and the destruction or capture of the garrison of Santiago, neither of which was pronounced by competent authority to be paramount; there were two commanders, the naval and the military, neither of whom had any authority over the other; and there were two sep-

---

* When this was written I was away from the regiment on leave of absence.

arate forces, one on sea and one on land, operating as far apart as they could well get from each other. It would carry me beyond the scope and compass of this work to indicate further than I have done the unfortunate consequences of thus violating the fundamental principles of the art of war. Moreover, the facts and figures, especially on the side of the enemy, are not sufficiently known to make a scientific study of the campaign possible. The official reports and returns of both armies, and accurate military maps of the theatre of war, both strategic and tactical, must first be available. This is not yet the case with our Civil War, which ended more than thirty years ago, although more than one hundred bulky volumes and a handsomely executed atlas have been published about it at an immense cost to the Government. But a fact important to the soldier and the citizen has been brought home to both, and that is that our military establishment is radically defective in its organization. It is generally expected that a bill to reorganize the army will be introduced and made a law in the course of the present or the next session of Congress. Reorganization may do a great deal towards preventing the bungling and suffering of our late war, but not everything. The efficiency of our army depends upon the spirit that flows into it through the Commander - in - Chief and his Secretary of

CONCLUSION

War from the body politic, upon the interest taken in the army by the people, which in turn depends upon the popular conception of the military necessities of the country, actual and prospective.

The vital principle of the vast military establishments of Europe is a general apprehension of war. For years past our people have thought of war only as a chimera, and our officers and soldiers have hardly taken military training seriously. If an army is to attain the highest degree of effectiveness, it must feel that it is liable any day to be ordered to mobilize for war. But rumors of war cannot be created and kept up at will. There are times, fortunately for mankind, when there cannot be any such sensation as a " war scare." Especially in such times must the impulse to military exertion come from the people. In periods of profound peace, public interest in the army is the first condition to professional interest within the army. This points to the need of close relationship between the army and the people, and suggests local recruiting, autumn manœuvres, and a general decentralization of our military administration. Decentralization and the practice of field manœuvres on a large scale are called for by other considerations. Decentralization is essential to prompt and vigorous action with masses of troops. Field manœuvres are indispensable not only to the proper training of an army but also to its proper inspection. As tests of efficiency of commanders and their commands, they should be the more severe, and the more rigorously applied the greater the decentralization.

The President has been criticised for certain military appointments made during the late war. But the President was elected by the people, and his appointments had to be confirmed by the Senate. Many if not most of the appointments referred to were made at the instance of Congressmen or of the people whom they represent. The responsibility for the short rations in Cuba, and sickness at Camp Wikoff, Camp Thomas, Camp Alger, Tampa, and other points rests for the greater part upon the people of the United States, in many cases upon officers and soldiers who suffered from them, and are now vociferous in censuring the Secretary of War and his chiefs of bureau.

Every man, woman, and child who ever gives a thought to the subject realizes that a civilian, inexperienced in war, is not competent to command an army, and an American can hardly reach the age of maturity without learning that the President is Commander-in-Chief of the army and navy, and that many, if not most, of our Presidents have been devoid of military training and experience. I have heard civilians who were interested in the state of the army say that

CONCLUSION

the President or the Secretary of War ought to be a military man. To this there is an insuperable obstacle in the old Anglo-Saxon principle that the civil power is superior to the military. As Secretary of War, a retired army officer would have about the same military aspirations and ambition as one in active service, without the latter's interest in the after effects of his administration. He would have the bad points of an officer in active service without his good points. A civilian who had, let us say, been at West Point, and served in the army, and was an up-to-date theorist in military matters, would be the more objectionable the more he made use of his military attainments, for any lawyer, politician, or gentleman of leisure who should succeed him would feel quite able to do what he did, and would undertake to do it. The first Secretary of War to assume the functions of commanding General was Jefferson Davis. Being a West Point graduate, and having served as an officer of the Regular Army, he proved himself one of the best Secretaries of War, perhaps the best, that we ever had. But the consequence has been that practically every Secretary of War since then has had to prove himself an indifferent commanding General. Civilian soldiers are a rarity. Their incumbency must be the exception rather than the rule, and therefore no system or policy can be securely based upon it.

But even if military talent and experience were common among our public men, those qualities would not be desirable in a Secretary of War, for the reason that is implied in the constitution, that military proficiency is inseparable from military ambition. In a Republican Secretary of War, military ignorance is not a fault, but a virtue; not a defect, but an essential qualification, provided that the Secretary of War appreciates his ignorance and governs himself and his department accordingly.

What is needed in a Secretary of War is genuine patriotism coupled with nobility and force of character. The Secretary of War is the main source, the fountain-head, of military virtue. He must make himself felt throughout the army by his self-sacrificing devotion to its highest interests, and command its admiration by his courageous resistance to the pressure of selfish politicians. It goes without saying that his military record, if he has one, should be a model to be held up to our officers and soldiers for their guidance and inspiration.

The fathers of the constitution must have realized that the President cannot, generally speaking, be a military expert, but they were resolved at any cost to insure the supremacy of the civil over the military power. They meant that the President should be responsible to the country for the loyalty and efficiency of the army

and navy, and realized that he could not be just-
ly held responsible therefor unless he had control of every officer and enlisted man in the two
services. The simplest, not to say the only, way
to give him this authority was to make him Commander-in-Chief.

It was intended that the President should at
all times be more civilian than soldier, that the
civilian side of him should always dominate the
military; that in his dual capacity of civil magis-
trate and Commander-in-Chief he should typify
the supremacy of the civil over the military
power. He is essentially a civilian, and, unless
he were, could not in accordance with the genius
of our Government be Commander-in-Chief. An
officer of the army is prohibited by law from
holding any civil office. The Commander-in-
Chief of the army and navy holds the highest
civil office of the government; and he cannot be
now a civil executive, and now a military; he
cannot for a moment divest himself of his civil
character. To do so would be to make the military power for the time being irresponsible, or
supreme. As well might the senior general
officer of the army be independent of or superior
to the President. It is proper that the President as Commander-in-Chief should be inscribed
in the "Army Register," but in no legal sense is
he an officer of the army. The President of the
United States and the governors of the states

review their troops in silk-hats and frock-coats. It would shock the political feelings of our people to see either in military uniforms, nor would they permit either to take command of troops in the field.

It was not intended that the President should regularly command the army or navy. His office, though nominally that of Commander-in-Chief, was intended to be virtually that of inspector, with provisional authority to act in emergencies as Commander-in-Chief. What he had chiefly to do in his military and naval capacity may be briefly stated as follows:

1. To inspect, or oversee, the army and navy.
2. To insure their harmonious co-operation.
3. To regulate their expenditures.

The latter duty is a corollary of another Anglo-Saxon principle, that the same hand that holds the sword shall not hold the purse-strings. This principle is violated just as much when the Secretary of War assumes the functions of General commanding as it would be were the General commanding to usurp those of the Secretary of War. Congress alone can furnish the money with which the President, as Commander-in-Chief, or his subordinates, can carry on war. The Commander-in-Chief, as a civilian, approves or disapproves of the estimates of his military and naval subordinates, allots and issues to them as he thinks proper the funds appropriated by Congress, and passes upon their accounts before they are transmitted to an auditor of the Treasury for settlement.

It is perhaps impossible to draw the line sharply between safe-guarding the liberties of the people and being a war lord. But do our presidents try even to stake out that line?

The organization of the army should embody the two ideas of supremacy for the civil power and unity of command and responsibility for the military power. I am impressed with the conviction that the War Department should be reorganized so as to consist of a Secretary of War, a number of Assistant Secretaries, and a force of civilian inspectors and clerks. The Secretary of War might represent the President, as he has represented him, so that an order from the Secretary should have the legal value of an order from the President. Under ordinary conditions the Secretary of War is a substitute for the President. I know there are officers who question the legality of this feature of our military government, but I see no objection to it. At any rate the Secretary and Assistant Secretaries should attend to the fiscal affairs of the army, the preparation of such orders as the President or Secretary of War might see fit to issue, and the commissioning of officers. Under the constitution the President is charged with the appointment of the officers of the army, " by and with the advice and consent of the Senate." In the performance of this duty he should be governed by the recommendations of the General commanding the army, except in such cases as may seem to him to tend distinctly to the subversion of the loyalty or efficiency of the army. The civilian inspectors should have duties generally similar to those of the late War Investigating Commission, and powers considerably greater.

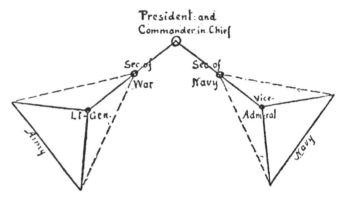

There should be the grade and office of Lieutenant-General commanding the army, a Great General Staff, and a General Staff—the Great General Staff to be subordinate to the Lieutenant-General commanding the army, and the General Staff subordinate to the Great General Staff. I have endeavored to outline the general plan graphically in the diagram.

The duties of the Great General Staff should be substantially those of similar organizations in

CONCLUSION

Europe: to gather and arrange for use all kinds of military information about our own country and foreign countries, to draw up plans of mobilization and operation, to search the records of our past wars for valuable data and useful lessons, to insure the harmonious and efficient co-operation of the several branches of the General Staff, and to direct the military education of officers and men, uniting the military academy, the post-lyceums, and service-schools into one system, and establishing a school or schools for non-commissioned officers. The General Staff should perform the military duties now performed by the Adjutant - General's department, Quartermaster's department, Commissary department, etc., the supply departments being consolidated or grouped under one head. The officers of these two staff organizations should form one corps, known as the General Staff Corps. Their names would be borne on one list for promotion. Appointments to the General Staff Corps should be based upon military ability, and its officers kept in sympathy with the line by rotation of duty between the staff and the line.

I wish it understood that I advocate these measures in combination and not separately. I would not answer for the working of one of them without the others. I should expect nothing but failure from a General Staff Corps which was not subordinated to the commanding General, or to which admission might be gained by marrying a Senator's daughter, or from which, once admitted, one would not have to return now and then to the line. To say in defence of our present system of continual service in the staff that the officers of our staff corps have on an average served twenty years in the line, and that therefore they are not lacking in familiarity with the needs of the line, is to ignore an important object of service in the line for staff-officers. A man who had been divorced from his wife after living with her twenty years would not care for her any more than if he had lived with her but ten, or five, perhaps not so much. If our general staff officers had all served one hundred years in the line, it would be no less important that they should occasionally return to it. It is one thing to know what the line needs, it is another to care whether it gets what it needs. General staff officers who are out of the line for good, who are never identified with it, are less sympathetic towards it, less zealous to supply its needs, than such as realize that they will sooner or later be in the line themselves, and may wish for the very supplies or methods which they are now asked to furnish or institute; that their distinction in war may depend upon the service that they render in the line, and so upon the efficiency of the line. The main purpose of having general staff officers serve in the line is to make them practically interested in the condition of the line.

Familiarity with staff work is essential to efficiency as a line officer, and so the general staff is a school for line as well as staff officers, and officers of the general staff corps serve indifferently in the line or in the staff. The terms *general staff* and *great general staff* are really misnomers. They might more properly be *general service* and *great general service*.

I have lying before me a copy of the *Army and Navy Journal* of November 19th, in which I read: "Some radical changes will be proposed [in Congress] in the system of staff departments. . . . The proposition which seems at present to be most in favor with military students is to remodel the staff departments in general on the German system, but we question whether it will be adopted, as there is no analogy between a chief of staff to a civilian President changed every four years and that of an Emperor trained to arms from his cradle and lifted above the jealousies and contentions that disturb the judgment of one subject to the limitations of our political system." My plan obviates the objection implied above, so far as it seems to me to have any force, by placing the general staff under the commanding General.

It has been asked: What is the use of a great general staff if the separate staff corps, as they now exist, are efficient? The question admits that these separate staff corps may not be efficient. A great general staff is recommended as a means of making and keeping them so. An important factor of efficiency in the separate staff corps is their relationship one to another, their harmonious co-operation, which depends upon unity of direction. I have heard it argued that the work of each of our present staff corps is a specialty, and that no single man can master the details of all the corps, and that, therefore, a great general staff cannot prove efficient. It is not necessary in order to regulate the several staff corps to be a specialist in each one. The mastering of the main points and principles of their several specialties must be feasible, or efficient command would be impossible. The great general staff officer needs a general knowledge of the specialties of the general staff. That general knowledge is his specialty.

The usefulness of the supply departments would be promoted by their subordination to officers who, at least for the time being, were independent of those departments, and authorized to determine the character of the supplies to be furnished.

Whether our infantry and cavalry should have magazine-rifles or single loaders, smokeless powder or black powder; whether they should charge with bayonets and sabres or with clubbed mus-

CONCLUSION

kets and revolvers; whether our horses should be furnished by contract or from depots; whether our rifles and carbines should be sighted so as to hit what they are pointed at or not; whether the revolver should have a smaller calibre than the rifle and carbine or a larger one, and other such questions, should be determined by officers competent to give due consideration to the interests both of those who have to use these articles and of those who have to furnish them. The determination of what supplies shall be furnished may require an impartial view both tactical and administrative to be taken of all branches of the service, and this can best be done from the office of a great general staff.

It is not to be expected that all the brightest and noblest minds in the army would be gathered into the general staff corps, nor is that to be desired. The superior fitness of general staff officers for their particular work would be a matter of education rather than of selection.

In the training of an army, uniformity is of extreme importance. When a captain gives the command, *Forward, march!* it makes little difference whether the men step off with the right foot or with the left, but it is important that they should all step off with the same foot. When he wants his company to change direction, it matters little whether he commands, *Right Turn!* or, *Right Wheel!* but it will not do for one captain to give one of these commands, and another the other. It is to prevent inconvenience and consequent confusion, as well as to prescribe in regard to many matters what is officially held to be the best view, that armies have drill regulations, firing regulations, general regulations, regulations for field - service, etc. But there are matters which lie outside of the domain of formal regulations, in which a certain uniformity is desirable or necessary. A commander can do more with a command the more he knows what it can do when called on, and what it will do when left to itself, or acting independently. The ability to reckon with commanders and their commands depends upon a knowledge of their mental and physical qualities, and this knowledge depends upon a certain uniformity in the training of officers and men. The knowledge is the harder to attain the higher the commander and greater the number of men, and it increases in importance about in the same ratio, for its importance is determined mainly by the degree of independence of the commanders in question. It is especially important that officers of the rank and position of chiefs-of-staff and commanding Generals should have been through a certain training in common, that they should have received from some single institution, if not one individual, impressions imparting to them a general unity of mind and charac-

tcr. Our highest officers come some from West
Point, some from the service-schools (Fort Leavenworth, Fort Monroe, Fort Riley, Willet's
Point), some from the Volunteers, some from the
ranks of the Regular Army, some from two or
more of these different schools. For uniformity and higher education among these officers
we need a military university, where the most
advanced discoveries of military science, both
theoretical and practical, are taught, and a competent body of investigators constantly engaged
in teaching. The navy has one in its War College. But no "service-school" can give the
training that is obtained by actual service in the
general staff. I need hardly add that it is not
to be had at an ordinary army-post. An officer
cannot find the time, books, documents, etc., to
say nothing of the guidance and inspiration necessary to the profitable pursuit of general staff
studies while serving with a regiment.

A general staff corps is the proper finishing
school for superior officers, completing the unifi-
cation as well as the development begun at the
military university. It would be generally recognized as the brains of the army, and its officers
as the proper persons to hold the high staff positions and commands. Any President, how much
soever he might be pressed or inclined to ignore
them for political favorites, would think a long
time before doing so. The general staff corps

would prove a check to the abuse of military patronage, and as such alone would justify its establishment and maintenance. No longer would Congressmen join the army to advance themselves as politicians, or army officers turn politicians, either in or out of the army, to better their military fortunes. Army officers would realize that the practise and study of their profession are the surest, if not the only road to military honors. What sort of spirit can be expected to animate a cadet or a student officer in an army which, on the outbreak of war, is expanded from twenty-five thousand to more than two hundred and fifty thousand men without the promotion of officers who have served from twenty-five to thirty years in the line, while youngsters hardly out of the cadet-school, and officers from the staff departments, from the retired list, and from civil life, are promoted above them?

The officers of our staff departments are guaranteed by law more promotion in time of peace than officers of the line. This has seemed to be justified by the theory that in time of war staff-officers are confined to their offices or overshadowed by their chiefs, and thus handicapped in competing with line officers for distinction and promotion. The principal argument by which our large staff establishment has been defended is that staff duties are particularly difficult and important, and that, on the expansion of our standing army to meet the condition of war, all our trained staff-officers would be needed in the staff. But we have seen in our recent war officers of the Adjutant-General's corps, the Inspector-General's corps, the Medical corps, and the Engineer corps take the field as full-fledged regimental brigade and division commanders, over the heads of officers of the line who had been drilling and studying and experimenting, under the impression that both the staff and the line were maintained in time of peace to insure their service, each in its proper sphere, in time of war.

It is a well-known fact that the officers stationed in Washington have a powerful, not to say controlling, influence upon legislation and public opinion concerning the army. The reports of the heads of departments are regularly communicated through the Secretary of War to Congress and through the press to the people. It is the officers in Washington who are most consulted by military committees, and who are the most active and successful in pressing their views upon individual Congressmen. It is, therefore, in the interest of wise military legislation that these officers be truly representative of the army in all its parts, and united in a perfect comprehension of the state and needs of the army. I can think of no better way of realizing this condition than the formation of an efficient general staff corps.

The chief expenditures of war may be grouped under three heads—money, blood, and time. A nation's military policy should be based upon a just appreciation of the relative values of these items. Our country is rich. We need not economize in money at the expense of either of the other items. As a people we are brave and patriotic. We shed blood freely for a cause of which we approve. But we set a high value on human life, and will not spend our own and our brother's blood as we will our money. We are an industrious, liberty-loving people. Apart from the sickness and death incidental to war, we object to a state of war on account of its interference with our business, and the strain to which it subjects our free institutions. Our wars may be ever so costly, but they must be short, if we can make them so without maintaining too large an army in time of peace. The danger to be feared from an army is twofold, physical and moral. In our country, a large army may do more harm by the influence of its deportment off duty and by and through its votes than it could with its bayonets and bullets.

The vote of a raw recruit counts for as much as that of a perfect soldier. Our army should be small and highly trained, rather than large and imperfectly trained. We want as few military citizens as possible, and we want our soldiers to share the thoughts and feelings of the people,

CONCLUSION

in short, to represent the people; but we want the army equipped and trained according to the latest and most approved ideas, with due regard to our national characteristics and institutions. We want it to be as strong as possible for the numbers. There is too much talk just now of increasing the army, and not enough of improving it. Our army might be strengthened thirty per cent. without adding an officer or a soldier to it.

The apportionment of the two factors of military power, numbers and discipline, is a fundamental problem in the reorganization of the army. In the interest of discipline it may be advisable to make a considerable increase in the Regular Army, but I doubt whether in time of peace our people will consent to maintain as large a standing army as would be necessary for order and security at home and in our colonies. Our military wants and necessities will be harder to figure on than heretofore. It will be necessary to have the means of promptly expanding the force which the people will consent to keep constantly in service. Our attention should therefore be directed to the perfection of the Volunteer force as a reserve for the Regular Army, giving it an organization and status for times of peace, and leaving the militia to perform those duties within their respective states and the United States which are exclusively contemplated for them in the constitution.

SANTIAGO CAMPAIGN

Our people are too much pleased with the result of our late war to be disposed to criticise the methods by which it was attained, and generally too ill-informed upon military matters to be able to appreciate the weakness of our military system. The great military reformations of this century, those of Prussia and France, were the consequences of crushing defeat and national humiliation. How is ours to come about?

Experience is a good teacher; there is none more thorough; but it is sometimes terribly severe and costly. We may get military wisdom, as France and Germany did, from bitter experience, but had we not better learn our lesson from the gentle muse of history?

No patching up of our military establishment will satisfy earnest and intelligent reformers. The radical changes which should be made in our War Department will never be instituted or initiated by the department itself. The impulse thereto must come from without, and it will not come until the essentials of military policy and institutions are taught in our colleges and public schools, or are brought home to us as they were to the Germans in 1806 and to the French in 1870.

THE END

Puerto de Bayamo · Coiba · Manantuaba · Alto · Villalon · S.

Sabana · Valiente Guao · El Caney

Miraflores · Cabanas · A. Sculcer

Paradis · Mirguero · SANTIAGO

Comancho · DE CUBA

R. Cobre

La Vega · San Juan Bay · S. Ursula · San Juan

RATON'S CAY · El Pozo · Sevilla

Pardino · S. Francisco · Aguadores · Las

Cabanitas · SMITH CAY

Mazamarra · Peluca

Cabana · Cave Battery · Sardinero · Siboney

Battery · MORRO CASTLE · Battery

Caballitas B. · Piedras Altas · LIGHT HOUSE · Aguadar · Sardinero · Rio Julio

C A R I B B E A N

SCAL. E MILES

ENGRAVED BY R. D.

SERVOSS, N. Y.

A MODERN HISTORY OF A MODERN WAR

HARPER'S PICTORIAL HISTORY OF THE WAR WITH SPAIN

holds an exceptional position to-day among modern literary wonders. Its high artistic qualities are unprecedented in modern printing, and it has established a standard in pictorial art that will be difficult to equal. The brilliant victories achieved by our soldiers and sailors have been faithfully pictured and described for this history by men pre-eminent in art and literature. No point of interest has been left uncovered.

INTRODUCTION BY MAJOR-GENERAL MILES, U. S. A.

A PARTIAL LIST OF CONTRIBUTORS

Caspar Whitney, Hon. John Barrett, Arthur Houghton, Sydney Brooks, Arthur Dutton, Max F. Klepper, Robert G. Butler, Harold Martin, Thomas R. Dawley, Jr., John Fox, Jr., C. E. Akers, Stephen Bonsal, George Bronson Rea, Clyde D. V. Hunt, F. M. Nadal, T. Dart Walker, R. Buenamar, Henry S. Richardson, F. D. Millet, Poultney Bigelow, J. F. Bass, Oscar King Davis, Carlton T. Chapman, General Frederick Funston, Frederic Remington, J. C. Frémont, Francis E. Leupp.

OFFICIAL ACCOUNTS OF CAMPAIGNS AND BATTLES

Generals Miles, Merritt, Shafter, Wheeler, Lee, Lawton, Chaffee, Kent, Hawkins, and others.

OFFICIAL ACCOUNTS OF NAVAL ACTIONS AND BOMBARDMENTS

Admiral Dewey; Rear-Admirals Sampson, Schley, Watson, and Philip ; Captains Clark, Evans, and Chadwick; and Commander Wainwright.

WOMAN'S PART IN THE WAR

Mrs. John A. Logan, Clara Barton, Anna Wheeler, Louise E. Hogan, Margaret Hamilton Welch, Alice Worthington Winthrop, Elizabeth M. Clark, Dr. Anita Newcomb McGee, and others.

THE RESULTS OF THE WAR

Territory that has passed under American influence ; vivid pen and pencil pictures of Cuba, Puerto Rico, The Philippines, Hawaii, etc. ; full descriptions of the Commercial Resources and Economic Conditions, etc., etc.

SOLD ONLY BY SUBSCRIPTION

Address

HARPER & BROTHERS, PUBLISHERS, NEW YORK CITY, N. Y.

By RICHARD HARDING DAVIS

A YEAR FROM A REPORTER'S NOTE-BOOK. Illustrated by R. Caton Woodville, T. de Thulstrup, and Frederic Remington, and from Photographs taken by the Author. $1 50.

THREE GRINGOS IN VENEZUELA AND CENTRAL AMERICA. Illustrated. $1 50.

ABOUT PARIS. Illustrated by C. D. Gibson. $1 25.

THE PRINCESS ALINE. Illustrated by C. D. Gibson. $1 25.

THE EXILES, AND OTHER STORIES. Illustrated. $1 50.

VAN BIBBER, AND OTHERS. Illustrated by C. D. Gibson. $1 00 ; Paper, 60 cents.

THE WEST FROM A CAR-WINDOW. Illustrated by Frederic Remington. $1 25.

OUR ENGLISH COUSINS. Illustrated. $1 25.

THE RULERS OF THE MEDITERRANEAN. Illustrated. $1 25.

Post 8vo, Cloth, Ornamental

Mr. Davis has eyes to see, is not a bit afraid to tell what he sees, and is essentially good natured. . . . Mr. Davis's faculty of appreciation and enjoyment is fresh and strong : he makes vivid pictures.—*Outlook*, N. Y.

Richard Harding Davis never writes a short story that he does not prove himself a master of the art.—*Chicago Times.*

HARPER & BROTHERS, Publishers
NEW YORK AND LONDON

☞ *Any of the above works will be sent by mail, postage prepaid, to any part of the United States, Canada, or Mexico, on receipt of the price.*

By WILLIAM DINWIDDIE

PUERTO RICO: Its Conditions and Possibilities. With 64 Illustrations. Crown 8vo, $2 50.

Mr. Dinwiddie has made a thorough study of the people, the climate, and the natural resources, and this book will be indispensable to every one who is considering Puerto Rico as a field for industrial enterprise. The business opportunities for Americans in sugar - cane, tobacco, coffee, and small fruits are set forth at great length.

Mr. Dinwiddie gives the most complete and satisfactory information as to the expense and the best methods of conducting coffee, sugar, and small - fruit plantations, as well as the opportunities offered to American investors in railroads, tramways, ice-plants, cattle-raising, dairy-farming, and manufacturing. The cost of living and the price of labor are all set forth in detail. In addition to its practical value as the best hand-book of Puerto Rican agriculture and manufacturing, the volume contains a full description of the natural resources, physical features, vegetable and mineral wealth, climate, prevalent diseases, and hygienic precautions for preventing them. It is the best book of its kind.

HARPER & BROTHERS, Publishers

NEW YORK AND LONDON

☞ *The above work will be sent by mail, postage prepaid, to any part of the United States, Canada, or Mexico, on receipt of the price.*

Made in the USA
Monee, IL
26 August 2024